6 —

3/102.

D0374966

BLOG

OTHER BOOKS BY HUGH HEWITT

First Principles

Searching for God in America

The Embarrassed Believer

In, But Not Of

If It's Not Close, They Can't Cheat

BLOG

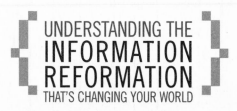

UNDERSTANDING THE
INFORMATION
REFORMATION
THAT'S CHANGING YOUR WORLD

HUGH HEWITT

NELSON BOOKS
A Division of Thomas Nelson Publishers
Since 1798

www.thomasnelson.com

Published in Nashville, Tennessee, by Thomas Nelson, Inc.

Published in association with Yates & Yates, LLP, Attorneys and Counselors, Orange, California.

Nelson Books titles may be purchased in bulk for educational, business, fundraising, or sales promotional use. For information, please e-mail SpecialMarkets@ThomasNelson.com.

All Scripture quotations, unless otherwise indicated, are taken from the New Revised Standard Version of the Bible (NRSV), copyright © 1989 by the Division of Christian Education of the National Council of the Churches of Christ in the USA. Used by permission.

ISBN 0-7852-1187-X [CIP to come]

Library of Congress Cataloging-in-Publication Data

Hewitt, Hugh, 1956-
    Blog : Understanding the information reformation that's changing your world / Hugh Hewitt.
    p. cm.
    ISBN 0-7852-1187-X (hardcover)
    1. Weblogs. 2. Mass media--Influence. 3. Online journalism. I. Title.
TK5105.8884H48 2005
    006.7--dc22

2004025938

Printed in the United States of America

05 06 07 08 09 QW 9 8 7 6 5 4 3 2 1

FOR BETSY

CONTENTS

CONTENTS

PART III
EARTHQUAKES, HURRICANES, AND TORNADOES—
WHAT'S AN EXECUTIVE TO DO?

PREFACE

I know you are busy. Perhaps you picked this book up at the air-
port because you've heard the word *blog* thrown around. You're
not sure what it means, or that it should mean anything to you.

Or perhaps someone down the organization chart gave it to
you with a Post-It note attached urging *"Read."* You are wondering, "What's 'blog' mean?"

Blog is short for weblog. *Log* means "diary," as in a captain's
log on a ship. *Weblog* means a diary of sorts maintained on the
internet by one or more regular contributors. Usually just one,
sometimes two or three, rarely more than three.

The first blog appeared in 1999. Give or take a year.

There are now more than 4,000,000 blogs. Think about that.
From 1 to 4,000,000 in five years.

Blogs first got noticed when they invaded the realm of politics and journalism in a big way. An entire universe of *poliblogs*
sprang up to do commentary on politics and, necessarily, about
media. These blogs raised huge sums of money for candidates,

changed the contours of citizen political participation, and altered the course of the 2004 presidential election. Another wave arose after 9/11, generally called *warblogs*. These bloggers took up their keypads out of the urgency born from rubble of that terrible September morning.

The warbloggers had huge traffic through the invasion and conquest of Iraq, but then it was the time for the poliblogs to gather strength and influence. A few people in 2003 had a glimmer of an idea that that might happen in 2004. One of them was not Dan Rather. He paid a very big price.

Rather in 2004 was a lot like Leo X in 1517. Leo was pope when Luther started hammering on the cathedral door. Leo didn't react in time. His business—the Roman Catholic Church—was badly damaged by his obtuseness.

You might be Leo. You could be the CEO or just a branch manager, doing fine work, moving through your earnings projections or your quarterly sales goals with a pace and a confidence that are the envy of your peers.

Or you could be the pastor of a good-sized suburban church with healthy attendance and plans for a fourth service. Or the manager of a rock-and-roll band that has just cut a CD. Or the GM of a Major League Baseball team.

No matter what you do or who you are, the information delivery systems in the United States have just experienced a revolution. That revolution is expanding to all corners of the world. Everyone is potentially a journalist, including your executive assistant and the messenger bike boy. Everyone could have a blog and a cell phone that can snap a picture of you to put on it.

You need to figure this out. You need to get ahead of it. So don't put the book down. Read it and everything else you can find on the subject.

More big waves of blogging expansion are coming, with a certain explosion around the time of the next nomination to the United States Supreme Court or the next terrorist outrage that actually occurs within the United States. You need to understand the incredible power of the blogosphere before that next expansion occurs.

Most folks know who Luther is. Not many people know who Leo X is. Because Luther overwhelmed Leo.

Don't be a Leo.

At the end of this book, if you want a handy list of which blogs to begin reading daily as an introduction to the medium, return to this summary and Google the names two paragraphs down for their Web addresses. Bookmark and read every day.

Blogs can be divided along a spectrum that begins with *pure aggregators* that simply point readers to key links, and *pure analysts* who simply write their views on crucial issues or events. I consult hundreds of blogs every week, but at this writing, I consult twenty blogs at least two or more times a day. I recommend them all to you as a starting point.

The best of the aggregators, though they also throw in analysis in usually terse comments:

Instapundit (www.Instapundit.com)

RealClearPolitics (RealClearPolitics.com)

Command Post (Command-Post.org)

The Corner (NationalReview.com/thecorner/corner.asp)

KerrySpot (NationalReview.com/kerry/kerryspot.asp)

Polipundit (PoliPundit.com)

The best of the analysts who also provide a lot of pointers:

PowerLine (www.PowerLineBlog.com)
The Belmont Club (www.BelmontClub.blogspot.com)
Roger L. Simon (www.RogerLSimon.com)
Little Green Footballs (www.LittleGreenFootballs.com)
Lileks (www.Lileks.com)
Captain's Quarters (www.CaptainsQuartersBlog.com)

And the best who mix analysis with theology:

Evangelical Outpost (www.EvangelicalOutpost.com)
Mark D. Roberts (www.MarkDRoberts.com)
Dr. R. Albert Mohler Jr. (crosswalk.com/news/weblogs/mohler)
John Mark Reynolds (www.JohnMarkReynolds.com)

For the flavor of the idiosyncratic but powerful humor-sarcasm-parody bloggers:

Fraters Libertas (www.FratersLibertas.com)
Cadet Happy (www.CadetHappy.com)
Scrapple Face (www.ScrappleFace.com)
Infinite Monkeys (www.InfiniteMonkeysBlog.com)

Enjoy your exploration of the blogosphere, and begin to adapt your organization to its indisputable power.

INTRODUCTION

Between 6:00 AM on September 30, 2004, and 6:00 AM October 1, 2004, more than 130,000 internet users visited **HughHewitt.com**. They did so because the first presidential debate between George W. Bush and John Kerry was conducted on the night of the thirtieth, and folks wanted my take on the pre- and post-debate political setting, as well as my continually updated analysis of the debate as it took place.

I believed George W. Bush had won the debate, and that John Kerry had committed incredible blunders. Very, very few pundits agreed with me. I was right. John Kerry's "global test," his proposal to sell nuclear fuel to Iran and to deal unilaterally with North Korea, his opposition to a new generation of American nuclear weapons, his dismissiveness of the Poles and other allies, and his lack of understanding of the nature of the terror network was initially cloaked in smooth phrases and an impressive demeanor, but the focus that follows these debates quickly came to bear on Kerry's answers, and he sank like the *Titanic* after the iceberg gashed its lower regions. My readers knew about this collision with facts within minutes of Kerry's answers as I posted the analysis in real time.

Four years earlier I had delivered commentary in short sentences over radio and television, but with interruptions, commercials, and shared time, it was difficult to offer an extended analysis of the Bush-Gore contests.

Four years earlier the blogosphere had appeared but was not widely used. As 2005 dawns, the blogosphere universe is expanding at a huge rate, and as my 130,000 visitors on debate day and night demonstrate, Americans want more than they are getting from television, radio, and newspapers. They want more information from sources that they trust, not the same-old same-old from Rather, Jennings, and Brokaw, and certainly not the unread editorials of relentlessly biased and increasingly irrelevant scolds like the editors of the *Los Angeles Times*.

"Life is a habit, Hughie. Life is a habit." Jerry Tardie has said this to me about a thousand times. Jerry was once a basketball coach, and a very successful one, at Mater Dei High School in Santa Ana, California. He speaks in coach talk, the repetitive, specific, motivational, and tutorial style that all good coaches use.

His point is that all human beings are creatures of habit. He's right, of course, which is why this book will have a huge impact across many fields. It brings the news that millions of people are changing their habits when it comes to information acquisition. This has happened many times before: with the appearance of the printing press, then the telegraph, the telephone, radio, television, and internet.

Now, however, the blogosphere has appeared, and it has come so suddenly as to surprise even the most sophisticated of analysts. My WordPerfect 11 software doesn't even recognize the word *blogosphere*, as I discovered on my return flight from New York to

California on the Saturday after the Republican National Convention in early September 2004, where a few dozen bloggers provided yet more evidence of the revolution under way in information acquisition. **Technorati (www.technorati.com)**, a must-use tool of navigation in the blogosphere, counts more than four million blogs in being as 2004 came to a close. That's a pretty big thing to miss for the folks over at WordPerfect. But lots of people are "missing" the blogs.

Each of the RNC bloggers saw our blogs—short for *weblog*, an online site that is updated by its author(s) frequently—attract tens of thousands of visitors every day during the convention. The same thing happened at the Democratic National Convention, where I also blogged. My heaviest traffic day at the convention was over sixty thousand, which then doubled by the time of the first presidential debate. This is called "exponential growth," and it is occurring across the blogosphere.

These numbers pale in comparison to, say, the FOX News Network's audience at any given minute. But unlike television viewers, most visitors to my site came because they believed I had something unique to offer them. They trusted me. *Blog* is a book about trust; how old media—mainstream media—lost it and how new media is gaining it.

At the convention I had an opportunity to interview for my radio show three of President Bush's most senior political advisers: Karl Rove, Matthew Dowd, and Karen Hughes. In addition to these Republican operatives, I interviewed Democratic National Committee Chairman Terry McAuliffe and was interviewed by lefty radio host Al Franken. I had all of these interviews transcribed and posted them at **HughHewitt.com**. Excerpts from all of them were then picked up by scores of other bloggers and zipped around the blogosphere, changing the perceptions of tens of thousands, perhaps hundreds of thousands, of the convention and the presidential race within which it was a milestone.

Every other blogger there—and the tens of thousands of bloggers who weren't but who were writing and analyzing the events—were doing the same thing. Millions and millions of words were being written and read by individuals with no or limited connections to old media. Every previous political convention had been dominated and in many respects shaped by old media, a consortium of left-of-center television networks and big newspapers, with the big three weekly newspapers thrown in. I am confident that no single member of old media interviewed the five individuals I've just named on air, and even if they did, their conversations with the ones they did meet were not transcribed in real time. People who trust me read my interactions and my questions and got unfiltered information from the president's side and a good dose of hilarious and ineffective spin from the two lefties.

They will return, these readers, as they have been returning since I launched the blog in early 2002. Since then I have had more than 10,000,000 visitors to my site. I am one of thousands of blogs, though one of the larger ones when it comes to traffic and links to other blogs.

Why does this visitor traffic matter? Because the visitors to my blog are a symptom of information users on the move. Information habits are all smashed up. First cable news, then the online versions of old media, and now the blogs have followed one after the other in the space of a handful of years. Each has crashed into the established habits of information acquisition, each time setting free millions of information users. MTV had done the same thing to the music business twenty years ago, and entertainment changed in a eye blink. Now news and information are undergoing the same radical transformation.

People's attentions are up for grabs. Trust is being transferred. If you or your business—or your faith, or your family—depend upon the steady trust of others in you, your institution, or your product, suddenly you are at sea. If you don't know this, you are in the position of General Motors or Coke when television arrived. Two years ago I would have sold a lifetime ad on my site for a couple of thousand bucks to defray the start-up costs. At this writing it is $1,000 a month. Given who reads the site, that is cheap, and it will go up soon. Marketing is in a new age.

It is actually much, much more radical than that, but the language of consumption and advertising is well understood. What is really going on is an information reformation similar in consequence to the Reformation that split Christianity in the sixteenth century. The key to that Reformation was the wide dissemination of Scripture among an increasingly literate laity. Today we do not have a canon, but we do have an appetite for information, the arrival of a new technology of distribution, and a million willing content providers. The old guard of old media is in a situation very similar to the Roman Catholic Church's situation when Luther arose to challenge the pope's authority. Once Luther's spark set the fire, the availability of editions of the Bible made the collapse of the Church's authority inevitable, though the struggle was long and often bloody.

The collapse of old media's authority isn't going to be bloody, but it sure is entertaining as the self-appointed tell the self-anointed that this is all very, very bad. "What will happen without editors and producers?" they wonder. Exactly what is happening and will continue to happen: free markets of information are driving decision-making in politics and soon will drive consumption decisions and institutional reputations. The ground is shifting so quickly that it is impossible to overstate the impact, even as it would have been impossible to overstate the consequence of the arrival of television.

This book is the result of a conversation I had with the publisher of my most recent book, *If It's Not Close, They Can't Cheat: Crushing the Democrats in Every Election*, Thomas Nelson Publishers' Jonathan Merkh. That book had done quite well, having appeared for six weeks on the *New York Times'* best-seller list for nonfiction, and reaching number six on Amazon. In the course of discussing my plan for a series of books—not including this one—I explained to Jonathan my theory of what the savvy publisher would be doing right now, which is developing a blog about books that became a must-stop in the world of reading and selling and buying books. I would find the best one or two writers among the publishing world's many fine scribblers, brand the site with their names or a great blog name, and pump resources into blog ads to let blogosphere know that a new blog was in town devoted to books. Then I'd start running blog ads for that publishing house's own books and buzzing that publishing house's own buzz. In short, I'd build the means of production of sales, which will be driving book sales somewhere in the near future. There is a *New York Times Review of Books* in blog form coming. Maybe two or three. It would be best to own it.

The key is speed. Once the habit is formed, it will be hard to shake, because time is so precious in this day and age. I visit thousands of blogs a year, but only a handful daily. That "handful" list is hard to change, and as with me, so with millions. There is a race under way to gain mindspace, to be part of the blogosphere reader's habit. The bad news is that some of us have a couple of years' head start. The very great news is that the growth curve for blogosphere use is enormous.

Which is why you have to read this book very quickly and distribute it to your senior leadership, then hold a few days' retreat to discuss what is going on. I have made it short so that you can absorb it on a plane ride or a couple of hours of closed-door time, and so that it is relatively cheap to acquire the necessary copies. When you go on the retreat, spend the extra bucks to bring along one or two or even three of the bloggers from the very large A team. I will charge you a fortune, but others are not so expensive. There is value in the conversation even if no experienced hands are along, but why convene a meeting to discuss music and leave all the composers at home?

Although I am thinking of my audience as senior and mid-level executives in business, government, the arts, the church, and especially in politics, if television affects your life, the blogosphere will as well and probably already has. Even if you are a week away from retirement, you will still want to leave a copy with your replacement as you head out the door, a sort of an advance "I told you so."

A word about the scoffers. I hear from them every day—*every day*. They think they have the internet figured out; they have a strategy; they don't see the sales; they don't care about amateurs; they even blog a little themselves, and they don't get the big deal. The best word they have is "triumphalism." "A little too much triumphalism in that point of view," the scoffer will say.

Well, John Kerry was probably a scoffer once as well. If he ever had a chance of being president, it ended not with the appearance of Swift Boat Veterans for Truth and the John O'Neill book *Unfit for Command*, but with the jump from a book and a few stories by outside-of-the-mainstream sources to a credible, detailed, sophisticated assault on Kerry's truth-telling brought about with regard to Kerry's "excellent adventures" in Cambodia tales. This was done by the blogosphere—specifically **Instapundit**'s Glenn Reynolds, Tom McGuire at **JustOneMinute** (**justoneminute.typepad.com**), the gents at **PowerLine,** John Hinderocker, Scott Johnson, and Paul Mirengoff—Ed Morrissey at **Captain's Quarters,** me, and a few others. We forced the story out farther and farther into the information mainstream, even as old media resisted covering it. When FOX News's Carl Cameron finally reported on the controversy over Kerry's very specific, very emotional, and very fictional accounts of his Christmas Eve spent in Cambodia in 1968, the Kerry campaign was obliged to recant those stories, and then all of Kerry's many fables were on the table. He never recovered from an August spent hiding from the Vets, their ads, and a relentless inquest conducted fairly and with lawyerly thoroughness within the blogosphere.

Kerry joined the *New York Times'* ex-editor Howell Raines and the Senate Republicans ex–Majority Leader Trent Lott as men who never knew what hit them. This trio was in turn joined by Dan Rather and the CBS team at *60 Minutes 2,* which got blown away by a blog swarm when Rather's team offered up fraudulent documents as evidence of President Bush's service record in the Texas National Guard. These brief histories of these four episodes—what I call "the founding myths of the blogosphere"—are within, but understand from the beginning of the book that the crippling of Kerry, the ruin of Rather, the exile of Raines, and the demotion of Lott occurred because of bloggers. It is that simple. They are powerful men either wounded or even driven from powerful positions by relative unknowns working around the clock in text but not in print.

If people like Kerry, Raines, Rather, and Lott can be humbled by the blogosphere, so, too, can you, your company, your movie, your church, your anything.

And matched to that destructive energy is a parallel but only dimly understood creative energy as well. This will fully arrive when the new geography settles and the new "trusted" bloggers emerge out of the scramble. Imagine the foresight of Robert Moses when it came to laying out Central Park, of William Paley as he set out to build CBS, of Gates and Microsoft—of Billy Graham when he figured out that crusades could work to change the world.

The blogosphere is evolving at an incredibly rapid pace, and a lot of the best mindspace is being claimed, but there remains incredible opportunity among hundreds of millions who have yet to figure out that there is a better way to gain information than watching the tube: quicker, more specific, more emotionally satisfying. The blogosphere is about trust. CNN lost the trust it once had and its fall has been sudden and shattering. FOX News is trusted by millions, so its numbers have shot up, much to the dismay of lefties who don't understand why viewers would trust FOX News.

If you can get this point, you will get the blogosphere. None of us have time to understand everything, so we have to trust surrogates. When it comes to medicine, we understand this completely. When it comes to finance, we sort of understand this if we have trusted a broker with money or an insurance salesman with a policy. When it comes to drafting a will, we trust the lawyer involved. The list goes on and on.

People don't trust the old media with anything like the old level of confidence. There are plenty of books out there that explain what happened, but it basically comes down to the left-leaning ideology that was always there and increasingly became so widespread, transparent, and arrogant as to repel half the country. If you want to argue the point, this book isn't for you. Go watch your DVD of *Fahrenheit 9/11* again. Trot down to the coffee shop to expound on corporate ownership of transnational media conglomerates. You don't have a clue, and you won't when the night is over. But you will be farther behind.

MSM ("mainstream media") went left. Into that void have come first Rush, then talk radio, then FOX News, and now the bloggers, and from that initial entry point of news and politics, they will move on other fields, from restaurant reviews to theater to books to car purchases. Since consulting them is cost-free except for time, they are a deadly threat to print enterprises which, while irreplaceable for some functions, are easily replaced for others, meaning declining circulation.

You have to be very dim indeed to be planning a career as a print journalist these days, or to be holding much stock in print-heavy companies such as the Tribune Company. Being CEO of Tribune Company is a lot like the job of being the most important bishop in Germany when Luther started hammering his theses to the Wittenberg cathedral's door.

Few have been as damaged by a loss of information consumer trust as CNN. Sitting in the Minneapolis airport waiting for my connecting flight, I listen to CNN practically beg the audience to trust it. In Times Square the week of the Republican National Convention, CNN's banner read "America's Most Trusted Network," as laughable an assertion of American car "quality" in the seventies. The airport show—with a big audience, as Hurricane Frances was approaching—was full of single-frame banners shouting out "Resources" and "U.S. Bureaus" and flashing pictures of CNN personalities with dramatic music in the background swelling, all leading to the declaration: "America's Campaign Headquarters." This has to reflect the same false bravado masking desperation that gripped the Vatican in Luther's heyday.

By contrast, FOX News's soaring viewership numbers—for the first time at a major party convention, the RNC's this summer past, a cable channel passed the networks for total audience—reflects the trust of the newly emancipated information consumer. "Fair and balanced" was home-run branding, because it telegraphed to the half of the country that thinks Carville is a partisan and Begala a nutcase, Aaron Brown a lightweight and Bill Schneider hopelessly tilted toward the left, that FOX News would not be a wholly owned subsidiary of the DNC.

CNN is never going to get back what it threw away when it failed to discipline itself, because Fox moved in and new viewing habits have formed. In fact, even FOX News has to be very vigilant about its people. Had Carl Cameron not broken the John Kerry not-in-Cambodia-on-Christmas-Eve-1968 story, FOX News would have risked its standing with its audience, wired as that audience was to the blogosphere's hunt for the details and for its complete vindication of the Swifties' claims on this point.

Brit Hume, perhaps the most serious and accomplished of the major anchors, proceeded to drive his program's pundits toward the Cambodia story night after night, reaffirming again and again to his audience that he understood the story and its significance—earning its trust again and again. Panelists Morton Kondracke and Fred Barnes helped Hume secure that trust by treating the story with respect.

Contrast this reaction with what happened when first a poster at **Free Republic (FreeRepublic.com)**, then the **PowerLine** team brought forward the question of forgery in the wake of CBS's *60 Minutes 2* story alleging that George W. Bush had received preferential treatment and had disobeyed a direct order to receive a physical. CBS refused to question itself, even after these two sources—quickly followed by my site, **KerrySpot** at **NationalReview.com**, **INDC Journal**, **RatherBiased**, **BeldarBlog (Beldar.org)**, **Instapundit**, **Little Green Footballs**, etc.—compiled a mountain of proof that the docs were fakes. CBS instead doubled down, and a former senior CBS exec went on TV to blast bloggers as anonymous scribblers working in their living rooms in pajamas, instantly giving rise to thousands of humorous references to pajamas, and the term "pajamahadeen" coined by **KerrySpot**.

The longer CBS persisted in its ruse, the more attention was devoted to the cover-up in the blogosphere, and then the mainstream media, until both ratings and affiliates of the network forced a retraction.

Dizzying speed marked each of the four episodes wherein the power of the blogs was flexed, and that speed will only accelerate.

Change isn't coming. It is here. Information is being absorbed in new and startlingly different ways from new, and until recently, unknown sources. Your customer, your congregant, your critic is changing. You need to think that through.

I will help.

BLOG

PART I
WHAT HAPPENED

BLOG SWARMS
AND OPINION STORMS

"Burying the lead" is a great sin of journalism. It means putting the most important fact in a story deep into the body of the story, where the average reader or viewer might miss it. The "lead" fact should "lead" the story. Don't bury the lead. Lead with the lead.

Many books bury the lead. In their earnest plodding along through the facts to support their conclusions, authors build and build toward a conclusion that most of their audience never reads. The attention span of most Americans—never long to begin with—is getting shorter and shorter. Authors cannot afford to hide their most important points in the back of the book.

So, to the conclusion, arguments to follow: When many blogs pick up a theme or begin to pursue a story, a blog swarm forms. A blog swarm is an early indicator of an opinion storm brewing, which, when it breaks, will fundamentally alter the general public's understanding of a person, place, product, or phenomenon.

Blog swarms formed around Trent Lott and Howell Raines in 2002 and 2003 respectively, around details of John Kerry's Vietnam service in August of 2004, and around Dan Rather's forged documents in September of 2004. Opinion storms followed.

There was no shared plan of attack among the blogs. There was no coordination between them and their allies in talk radio and a few corners of MSM such as FOX News. There was, however, a network and there was an understanding of what mattered—facts—and a desire for speed and, crucially, a target. The destructive energy of the blogosphere is fierce indeed when focused.

This development could also have been predicted by anyone who followed the work of John Arquilla, a leading theorist of war and conflict. Arquilla has written extensively on "netcentric" warfare, and his books are available on Amazon and should be read by anyone in any competitive situation. The best summary article on netcentric warfare was written by Arquilla and coauthor David Ronfeldt for *Aviation Week & Space Technology* on September 29, 2003, and is reproduced with permission here:

> Technological advances often give rise to new types of weapons, but the achievement of lasting breakthroughs in fighting power requires organizational and doctrinal innovation as well. Invention of the internal combustion engine more than a century ago, for example, led to the tank and airplane. Yet these weapons systems did not realize their potential until the 1930s, when the Germans concentrated their armor into panzer divisions and articulated a blitzkrieg doctrine that tightly coupled maneuver forces on the ground with attack aircraft above. Today, the U.S. military is fielding awesome new technologies, but it is still far from figuring out the right organizational structures and doctrines for best applying them.
>
> Advanced information technologies have revolutionized U.S. forces' abilities to communicate swiftly, monitor enemy

movements in real time, operate vehicles remotely—on land, at sea, or in the air—and guide weapons in a way that effectively decouples range from accuracy. Yet, only modest attempts at organizational and doctrinal innovation have been tried.

The U.S. Air Force is experimenting organizationally by creating "composite" wings and tailored "air expeditionary forces" that mix different types of air platforms in the same tactical combat units. A concomitant new doctrinal emphasis on supporting advanced ground operations is bringing modern air power tantalizingly close, after so many decades, to realizing its fullest war-winning potential. The Marines have also engaged in field exercises in which the units of maneuver have been radically altered by creating autonomous units as small as eight-man squads. The Marines (not to mention special operations forces) understand that connectivity coupled with air mastery greatly empowers even the smallest combat formations.

For the most part, though, the bulk of the U.S. military is still wedded to heavy ground divisions and aircraft carrier battle groups. Almost all the technological changes of the past two decades have been folded into the Pentagon's existing understanding of war, summed up in the doctrine of "AirLand Battle." This concept of operations—originally intended for use against Russian forces if the Cold War ever got hot—is but a small upgrade to the aforementioned World War II-era blitzkrieg doctrine. Indeed, Norman Schwarzkopf's "left hook" in the Iraqi desert in 1991 was a virtual clone of Erwin Rommel's panzer sweeps across the North African desert in 1941.

Meanwhile, the world keeps moving into the age of networks. Networking means much the same for the military as it does in business and social-activist settings, not to mention

3

among information-age terrorists and criminals: monitoring the environment more broadly with highly sophisticated sensors; expanding lateral information flows; forming and deploying small, agile, specialized teams; and devolving much (but not all) command authority downward. But it also has a doctrinal implication that these other types of actors are learning faster than the U.S. military: It's a good idea to become adept at "swarming."

Swarming is a seemingly amorphous but carefully structured, coordinated way to strike from all directions at a particular point or points, by means of a sustainable "pulsing" of force and/or fire, close-in as well as from stand-off positions. It will work best—perhaps it will only work—if it is designed mainly around the deployment of myriad small, dispersed, networked maneuver units. The aim is to coalesce rapidly and stealthily on a target, attack it, then dissever and redisperse, immediately ready to recombine for a new pulse. Unlike previous military practice, battle management is now mainly about "command and decontrol," as networked units all over the field of battle (or business, or activism, or terror and crime) coordinate and strike the adversary in fluid, flexible, nonlinear ways.

Early examples of swarming appeared with the great mounted armies of the 7th century Muslims and the 13th century Mongols, both of which mastered the technique of omnidirectional attack. In modern times, British fighter planes swarmed from dispersed airfields all over southeastern England to harry massed Luftwaffe formations during the Battle of Britain, while at sea German U-boats were widely distributed when scouting, then converged to attack allied convoys. What's different today is that advanced sensing, communication and weapons guidance technologies make swarming possible in any terrain, against any opponent, 24/7.

While the American military remains officially wedded to AirLand Battle, its latest field campaigns exhibit the beginnings of a potential "BattleSwarm" doctrine. In Afghanistan in the fall of 2001, slightly more than 300 special forces soldiers, who were networked with each other and with various air-based attack assets, quickly toppled the Taliban. These same elites did it again in much of Iraq, striking all over the country from the outset, saving the oilfields in the south, knocking out the Scud Box in the west, coordinating with the Kurds in the north, and securing the approaches to Baghdad.

Will the U.S. military build on these first steps toward developing a truly networked "swarm force"? To best counter the adversaries bedeviling us in Iraq and Afghanistan, and those we may confront in other terror-war theaters, it is advisable to innovate along these lines. Right now, many military leaders are attracted to the concept of "network-centric operations," a vision of wiring together all our sensors and shooters. In some circles, however, swarming is being viewed narrowly, as a specialty notion, associated mainly with the use of autonomous (i.e., artificial intelligence-driven) systems. But as a deeper vision emerges and fixations on technology ease, serious questions will be raised about how best to give network-centric concepts operational life through organizational and doctrinal innovation. When these systemic questions get some traction, it will become evident that swarming is a big part of the answer.

All of this short article is directly applicable to any sort of conflict or competition, whether for a consumer's allegiance, a political candidate, or a religious belief. Part of succeeding either in the ascendancy of a brand, a candidate, or a cult is the destruction of the opposition. Blogging has been demonstrating for two years its destructive energy, and it is beginning to show its building potential as well, as demonstrated by the Northern Alliance of Blogs in Minnesota, which has coalesced, matured, founded a radio show, attracted sponsors, hosted events, and boosted candidates and events. Then two of them, **Captain's Quarters** (**CaptainsQuartersBlog.com**) and **PowerLine**, were credentialed to the Republican National Convention. Then those two plus **Lileks** (**Lileks.com**) helped bring national attention to the Christmas-not-in-Cambodia Kerry debacle. Then **PowerLine**, with a prompt from **Free Republic** and assists from **Little Green Footballs** (**www.LittleGreenFootballs.com**) and others in the blogosphere brought down Dan Rather.

It is thus the destructive power of the blogs that has got to be first on the mind of a reader. A senior journalist for the *Los Angeles Times* told me in the middle of "Rathergate" that he writes with the fear that he will be "blogged," meaning exposed as careless or agenda-driven, thus mocked and shamed and perhaps fired.

That fear—a good thing for journalists to carry with them—should also be on the minds of every public figure and corporate leader. If you aren't persuaded, spend some time studying the four episodes that brought the blogosphere to the attention of the nation. Details of each of the narratives differ according to whom you ask, because that's the nature of the blogosphere. With thousands of blogs pursuing a story, credit for a particular advance in the story may not get shared properly. Simultaneous breakthroughs are not only possible, they appear to be routine. Which is one way of saying to the bloggers reading this that if your name has been omitted, it wasn't intentional. A comprehensive treatise of the four founding myths of the blogosphere will have to await some grad student somewhere

Two of these episodes—the exposing of John Kerry's claim to have spent Christmas Eve in Cambodian waters in 1968 and the chronology of Rathergate—were first extensively chronicled by Jonathan Last of the *Weekly Standard*, who serves as the editor of the *Daily Standard*, and thus as my editor. We disagree as to some details and emphases, but Last certainly gets credit for being among the first to attempt to chart a news story's travels through the far reaches of the blogosphere. "What Blogs Have Wrought," from the September 27, 2004, issue of the *Weekly Standard*, and "The Not-So-Swift Mainstream Media" from the September 6, 2004, issue are the first two examples of blog archaeology, where a MSM writer goes back through the blogs to chart a story's evolution in details. Last, himself a blogger at **Galley Slaves** (**galeyslaves.blogspot.com**), has thus helped pioneer an MSM specialty—blog watching.

There will be many more such stories in the future, because there's no turning back on the open-source journalism power in the new media. For those who need reminding, here are my admittedly incomplete summaries.

THE TOPPLING OF TRENT

James Strom Thurmond was born on December 5, 1902, in Edgefield, South Carolina. One hundred years later, he marked his retirement from serving that state with a birthday party at the Dirksen Senate Office Building in Washington, D.C. Strom Thurmond had served forty-eight years in the Senate, longer than any other senator, and was its first centenarian. Longevity had been something of a theme throughout his life, including a twenty-four-hour filibuster in 1957, also the longest ever.

In addition to the many South Carolina supporters, Washington dignitaries, Senate colleagues, and Bush cabinet members in attendance at Strom's one-hundredth-birthday party were the usual journalists who covered congressional matters (Congress itself was out of session) as well as a few reporters from the cable networks and major newspapers, which had human-interest stories on the party planned for their morning editions. In addition, C-SPAN broadcast the proceedings on TV. "News" was not expected from the event, and none was reported. Initially, that is.

Senator Trent Lott of Mississippi, the once and future majority leader, was among the speakers. Lott grew rather serious at one point in his remarks and pronounced: "I want to say this about my state: When Strom Thurmond ran for president, we voted for him. We're proud of it. And if the rest of the country had followed our lead, we wouldn't have had all these problems over all these years, either."

Oops. Certainly, this was a fine compliment to give a man who devoted his life to politics. It even might have been received with acclamation in other circumstances. But the problem was that Strom Thurmond had run for president in 1948 on the States Rights' Democrat, or "Dixiecrat," ticket, which was based on the following promise: "All the laws of Washington and all the bayonets of the Army cannot force the Negro into our homes, our schools, our churches." According to one observer, Lott's apparent reminiscence for the days of segregation was followed by "an audible gasp and general silence." Lott resumed the festive mood after that inconvenient slip, and it seemed that nearly everybody present had soon forgotten. Everybody, that is, except for *ABC News* reporter Ed O'Keefe.

"When I heard [the comment]," recalled O'Keefe, "I thought, that didn't sound right; that couldn't have been in his prepared remarks." O'Keefe tested the waters by contacting the ABC congressional correspondent Linda Douglass, who called different organizations, such as the NAACP and the Leadership Conference on Civil Rights, which might have wanted to issue a response to Lott's statement. In addition, O'Keefe spoke with fellow reporters in attendance, but none thought all that much about Lott's comments. Douglass also turned up very little by way of a condemnation. All in all, the consensus seemed to be that this was not a story, and its absence from the news items covering the party reflected this sentiment.

O'Keefe's efforts were not completely in vain. *ABC News* did mention Lott's comments twice the following morning. At 4:30 AM, *World News This Morning* aired the comments and referred to a negative reaction by Wade Henderson of the Leadership Conference on Civil Rights, but then moved on. Later that morning, **ABCNews.com** posted the comments halfway down its hugely influential and lengthy daily news briefing, "The Note." Then the "story," if it could be called that, appeared to die a D.C. death.

Except that the then largely anonymous blogger, Atrios, had mentioned Lott's comments on his blog **Eschaton** (**atrios. blogspot.com**) at 1:21 PM on the sixth, simply stating, "Since political correctness is the scourge of society, I won't mention that the problems Lott is referring to are the Civil and Voting Rights Acts." Two hours later, Joshua Micah Marshall, a D.C.-based writer for the *Washington Monthly* and *The Hill*, was the second to post about the comments on his blog, **Talking Points Memo** (**www.talkingpointsmemo.com**): "There's a sort of agreement in Washington these days—with Thurmond's retirement and hundredth birthday—to sort of forget about all that unpleas-antness . . . Oh, what could have been!!! Just another example of the hubris now reigning among Capitol Hill Republicans."

Glenn Reynolds, of **Instapundit**, had picked up the growing Trent Lott story from Atrios and Marshall, also on the sixth. After somewhat forgiving Thurmond's segregationist past, at least for the duration of a hundredth-birthday celebration—which he compared to "youthful flings with Marxism"—Reynolds unapologetically laid into Lott: "But to say . . . that the country would be better off if Thurmond had won in 1948 is, well, it's proof that Lott shouldn't be Majority Leader for the Republicans, to begin with. And that's just to begin with. It's a sentiment as evil and loony as wishing that Gus Hall had been elected."

Also in the evening of December 6, Atrios posted an image of the official Democratic Party sample ballot from the 1948 presi-dential election. The ticket is forthrightly racist, declaring that if Mississippians allowed Truman to get nominated, "the vicious FEPC—anti-poll tax—anti-lynching and anti-segregation pro-posals will become the law of the land and our way of life in the South will be gone forever."

It is often possible—outside of campaign season—to forgive a gaffe. Elected officials, like all human beings, say stupid things every day. On the surface, Lott's remarks seemed merely to be one of these daily stupid utterances, especially to those not very famil-iar with the Dixiecrat platform or with Thurmond's mid-century politics.

But once the explicit racist agenda of the Dixiecrats was laid bare, any remark that appeared to allude favorably to "those days" rightly becomes so awful as to instantly move it beyond the realm of gaffe and into the realm of the unforgivable. Ignorance of the platform of the Dixiecrats was the reason given for some reporters' failure to realize that Lott's remarks were big news. But the blogosphere quickly provided the public (and those in the media watching) a crash course in segregationist politics and the full import of what Lott had said.

Thomas Edsall, of the *Washington Post*, ran an item on the Lott remarks on page six of the Saturday paper, but that was MSM's reaction: ho hum. Conservative commentators were not so easily quieted. Said William Kristol, editor of the *Weekly Standard*: "Oh God," he said, after learning of Lott's remarks. "It's ludicrous. He should remember it's the party of Lincoln."

Joshua Micah Marshall posted again on the story on December seventh. Atrios had follow-up posts as well. Atrios had begun to dig deeper into Lott's past at this point, posting a picture of Lott with members of the Council of Conservative Citizens. In 1992, Lott delivered a keynote address to this group and said the following, interpreted by many to apply to segregationist policies about white supremacy: "The people in this room stand for the right principles and the right philosophy. Let's take it in the right direction and our children will be the beneficiaries." The liberal bloggers had now begun to undergird their original disgust at Lott's remarks with solid information, forgotten by most, about the segregationist past and about Lott's longtime romanticism of it. And not just the bloggers of the left. On December 8, Glenn Reynolds made the most apt observation so far: "Seems the Blogosphere is way ahead on this one. Where's everybody else?"

Throughout the weekend, the blogosphere had already begun to "flood the zone," as journalists called it. Daniel Drezner, a University of Chicago law professor and uber-blogger, called for Lott's resignation on Saturday: "If Senate Republicans allow him to stay on as Majority Leader, they will deserve whatever political misfortunes befall them as a result . . . Senator, I say this as a Republican—do all of us a favor and get off the national stage."

Other bloggers of all political stripes began to call for Lott's resignation, including Josh Chafetz of **OxBlog** (**oxblog.com**), Virginia Postrel of **Dynamist** (**dynamist.com/weblog**), and Matt Yglesias, who wrote, "I'd like to think that both political parties could abide by a rule stating that folks expressing nostalgia for Jim Crow shouldn't be elevated to the highest ranks of power and influence." But perhaps the most stinging of these demands came from then-conservative blogger Andrew Sullivan. In the early hours of the morning on December 9, he gave the Republican Party a simple choice: "Either they get rid of Lott as majority leader; or they should come out formally as a party that regrets desegregation and civil rights for African-Americans." Sullivan also wondered why the story was getting so little coverage outside the blogosphere: "Why are the Republican commentators so silent about this? And the liberals? And where's the *New York Times*?"

Sullivan, like most other bloggers, seemed almost baffled by the general silence. Radley Balko later wrote a column for FOX News explaining the reticence on the part of major politicians, both Republican and Democrat, to criticize Lott—the reason being that the Senate is "an exclusive club where the collegial atmosphere causes otherwise smart people to give one another benefits of doubts to a fault." Even more likely, however, is that both parties did not like the implications of the story. Sure, the Democrats could assail Trent Lott and Republicans as racists; but unfortunately, it would then come up that actually Strom Thurmond was a Southern Democrat in 1948, like Robert Byrd, like the sainted Sam Ervin, like Al Gore Jr.'s father, Al Gore Sr., segregationists all.

In fact, one blogger created a test called the "20th Century History Final," which asked a series of questions such as, "Jim Crow laws were passed by legislatures controlled by . . . ?" "In Arkansas, the governor who stood in the door of a schoolhouse to block integration was a . . . ?" and "When the Rev. Martin Luther King Jr. led the civil rights efforts in the South, the governing powers that opposed him were of which party?" The answer, of course, to all of these questions is "Democrats."

One prominent Democrat, Senator Tom Daschle, went so far as to excuse the remarks: "Senator Lott, in my conversation with him this morning, explained that that wasn't how he meant them to be interpreted. I accept that. There are a lot of times when he and I go to the microphone, would like to say things we meant to say differently, and I'm sure this is one of those cases for him, as well."

Although some Democrats did speak up, notably, Al Gore and Jesse Jackson, the Party itself remained mostly silent.

Despite this widespread silence, the conservative Bible, the *National Review,* was all over the story on its blog, **The Corner,** where Jonah Goldberg had the following to say: "On the facts, Lott's comments were dumb. Morally, they were indefensible. Politically, they served to confirm the suspicions of millions of blacks and liberal whites about what is in the hearts of conservatives and Republicans . . . So tell me, What is he good for?"

In addition, David Frum, also of the *National Review,* noted that he believed Lott's remarks were intended to be "nothing more than a big squirt of greasy flattery" but went on to say that "what came out of his mouth was the most emphatic repudiation of desegregation to be heard from a national political figure since George Wallace's first presidential campaign. Lott's words suggest that one of the three most powerful and visible Republicans in the nation privately thinks that desegregation, civil rights, and equal voting rights were all a big mistake."

The initial clarification was given by Lott's pressman, Ron Bonjean, and was not nearly sufficient to answer the charges that had been circulating on the blogosphere. What was necessary was an apology that equaled full prostration. The apology that Lott finally did give on December 10, which would later become known as the "non-apology apology," fell far short of the expected standard, but it did launch the media blitz that would take up the conversation percolating in the blogosphere over the weekend and turn it into a lead story for the next few weeks.

The *Washington Post*, which had done the most in-depth stories so far, followed with two more on December 10, one by Thomas Edsall and the other by Howard Kurtz. In Kurtz's column "Why So Late on Lott?" the blogosphere got noticed. (Kurtz is by far the most blogosphere-savvy of the big names in MSM.) Kurtz wrote, "Trent Lott must go! That, at least, is the consensus of online pundits. What, you weren't aware that the Senate majority leader was in hot water for appearing to embrace the segregationist cause? Perhaps that's because, until this morning, most major newspapers hadn't done squat on the story."

Kurtz went on to pull quotes from Andrew Sullivan, Josh Marshall, David Frum, and Virginia Postrel. In addition, James Taranto's "Best of the Web Today" (hosted by the *Wall Street Journal's* website) jumped on the story. The piling-on effect had begun, and now, bloggers had an ally in the mainstream media. Together, they would push the story until Lott was gone.

For the blogosphere, the most important part of the Trent Lott affair was being noticed and credited by the mainstream media. Taranto helped to bring this about when he chided Paul Krugman—whom Taranto derisively called the "columnist of the year" (referring to an award Krugman had received)—for apparently lifting parts of his column from Josh Marshall. In his *New York Times* op-ed, Krugman wrote, "At first the 'liberal media' . . . largely ignored this story. To take the most spectacular demonstration of priorities, last week CNN's '*Inside Politics*' found time to cover Matt Drudge's unconfirmed (and untrue) allegations about the price of John Kerry's haircuts." Marshall himself did not seem to mind the lack of attribution from Krugman, but when Marshall unearthed an amicus brief that Lott had filed on behalf of Bob Jones University to maintain federal funding despite its intolerance of interracial dating, the Associated Press ran the story without giving credit to Marshall.

This is an unforgivable sin within academia and ought to be so within journalism: "One other thing," wrote Marshall. "Next time the AP rips off a story we broke at 11 AM and runs it as their own story at 5 PM maybe they could toss in a little attribution?" Marshall did get credit, however, from the *Dow Jones Newswires* report of the unearthed amicus brief. In addition, in another opinion column written on December 13, Krugman would mention Marshall: "'Right now we're debating whether the Republican Senate majority leader is a racist who yearns for the days of segregation or just a good ole boy who says a lot of things that make it seem like he's a racist who yearns for the days of segregation.' So writes Joshua Marshall, whose **talkingpointsmemo.com** is must reading for the politically curious, and who, more than anyone else, is responsible for making Trent Lott's offensive remarks the issue they deserve to be."

Once a *New York Times* columnist, even an unbalanced, frothing *New York Times* columnist, had acknowledged the presence of the blogosphere, it had been officially welcomed into the world of acceptable sources by MSM. The blogosphere would not, however, be content to be "a source," and ironically, the *New York Times* would itself be the next target of the gathering power of the blogosphere.

The rest of the Lott saga is already history. More and more damaging information came out. President Bush condemned the remarks, and black conservatives like Armstrong Williams joined in the call for Lott's ouster as majority leader. Lott's appearance on Black Entertainment Television, where he vouched unconditional support for affirmative action, had the effect of destroying any support he had within conservatives who despised the attempt to trade principles for personal position. Lott resigned before Christmas but stayed in the United States Senate and has begun a patient and disciplined rehabilitation. He may yet break Thurmond's record for longevity. If he does, it will be because he understands that the blogs are to be carefully watched and accounted for.

Bloggers quickly concurred that they could never have brought down Lott without the help of MSM. According to Marshall, the twenty-four-hour-news cycle of the mainstream media requires that a story "catch fire," and if it does not, "there's no second chance." However, despite the fact that the Lott story "clearly failed that first audition . . . [blogs kept] the ball in the air for a long enough time for people to realize that this was a much bigger story than people had understood." Atrios noted that "if Glenn Reynolds hadn't taken a stand on this story, then no one would have considered the role of bloggers . . . It isn't because Glenn was the first or the most vocal. Rather it was because he has a big megaphone and real media connections." In fact, Reynolds was one of the most vocal. On December 8, for example, ten of Reynolds's fifteen posts concerned Lott, and for the week thereafter, so did roughly half his posts. For a blogger who posts as much as Reynolds, this certainly qualifies as flooding the zone. The blogosphere, because of its relentlessness, had forced a story upon the MSM.

BLOWING UP THE TIMES

After the blogosphere made its first splash in the flood that drowned Trent Lott, the consensus among the media and the bloggers was that a healthy alliance between the two could effect major institutional change. The reason for this is that while bloggers could keep a story alive and even dig a little deeper, the media had the resources and the "big megaphones" necessary to make a story truly happen. In addition, the MSM believed it alone had the respect inherent in age-old institutions of information dissemination, institutions that people still trusted to deliver honest, fact-checked reports.

When the *New York Times*, the nation's "newspaper of record," was informed by the *San Antonio Star Express* on April 29, 2003, that one of its star young reporters, Jayson Blair, may have plagiarized material, a chain of events got under way that defined the blogosphere as an accountability mechanism for the media in the same way it had functioned as the accountability police in the Lott affair. In the aftermath of the *San Antonio Star Express* revelation, Blair resigned, on May 1, 2003, and apologized the next day. It was not immediately apparent that it was the sort of news that would shatter the *Times*'s power structure.

It was not as though something like this had never happened before. As John Ellis of **Tech Central Station (techcentralstation.com)** put it, "The Jayson Blair scandal was, on one level, a non-event. He lied, he got caught, he got fired." Five years earlier, negative stories about the scandal might have continued to run in competitive newspapers for a week or two thereafter, and a couple of exposés might have appeared on the major television networks. Seminars would have been scheduled at the journalism schools. Think pieces would have appeared in the *Atlantic Monthly* and *Harper's* a year later. And eventually, Blair would have emerged with a book and a speaking circuit gig for life.

That was then. Now, in 2003, after the story broke, Ellis wrote, "The blogs have talked of nothing else." It was an opportunity for new media to get its digs in. Blogger Richard Bennett best expressed the feeling of the blogosphere: "The media establishment has told us that responsible news organizations are more reliable than the blogs because of all these editors and fact-checkers, but who seriously believes that a blogger doing what Blair did could have survived more than a few months without being caught out? I sure don't." Mickey Kaus, an early uber-blogger whose **Kausfiles** (**Kausfiles.com**) is now part of **Slate**, observed that the *New York Times* and a blog are actually not at all alike: "One obsessively reflects the personal biases, enthusiasms and grudges of a single individual. The other is just an online diary!"

The blogosphere's love of hating the *Times* did not begin with Jayson Blair. *Times* editor Howell Raines brought out the worst in many bloggers, and thus their best blogging. Raines's arrogance and his liberalism were widely believed to have taken the *Times* into a new era of hyper-bias. One blog, **TimesWatch** (**TimesWatch.org**), was devoted solely to charting the paper's excesses.

TimesWatch was one of the first into the fray surrounding Blair and was relentless in its pursuit of "scalps" for the blogosphere. It became clear early on that the Blair controversy was not simply the case of another lying reporter. On May 2, 2003, the *New York Times* contained an editor's note on its corrections page mentioning that Jayson Blair had resigned (the last of many Blair-related corrections) as well as a news story about the scandal. Howard Kurtz of the *Washington Post* wrote that the paper had "run 50 corrections on [Blair's] stories." **TimesWatch** quickly did the math: "That's an average of one printed correction for every 14 stories that Blair wrote. Apparently, the editorial desk long overlooked the warning signs that not all Blair's work was 'fit to print.'" This was not a story about a luckless reporter who got caught plagiarizing once; this was a story about systemic editorial negligence at the foremost newspaper in the country. And it was just beginning.

Inside the *Times*, long knives came out, and the blogosphere provided a place where Raines's enemies could air their complaints. Jim Romenesko maintains a "neoblog" at **Poynter Online** (**Poynter.org**)—a highbrow/high-influence internet site devoted to journalism, within which Romenesko maintains a column of regularly updated entries, making his postings a neoblog in that it is a blog within an institutional structure. Romenesko's rolling report provided the discontented of the *Times* a place to vent their anger and to leak internal memos that would further discredit the upper management. Starting on May 2, the day Blair's resignation was announced, the "Letters Sent to Romenesko" ran the gamut of blame, from Affirmative Action to negligent management to personal responsibility. Some days it seemed that everyone inside and outside the *Times* had an opinion and an insatiable curiosity to see what would come of the scandal.

Much of the immediate speculation concerned whether Blair was artificially elevated to important assignments, such as the D.C.-sniper case, merely because he was an African American. Mickey Kaus, one of the first to address this issue, blogged that "the NYT apparently has run a minority internship program that has the effect . . . of hiring minority reporters right out of college . . . Blair seems to have been hired by the *Times* (after an internship) before he even graduated from college."

The question of race moved to center stage. On May 8, National Public Radio's Melissa Block interviewed Raines on her show *All Things Considered* and caught him off guard with an inconvenient quote of his:

> Mr. Raines, you spoke to a convention of the National Association of Black Journalists in 2001, and you specifically mentioned Jayson Blair as an example of the Times spotting and hiring the best and brightest reporters on their way up. You said, "This campaign has made our staff better and, more importantly, more diverse." And I wonder now, looking back, if you see this as something of a cautionary tale, that maybe Jayson Blair was given less scrutiny or more of a pass on the corrections to his stories that you had to print because the paper had an interest in cultivating a young, black reporter.

Needless to say, **TimesWatch** and **Kausfiles** were all over this, with Kaus tersely questioning, "'Better'? More importantly, 'more importantly'?"

It became apparent within the paper that a further explanation was needed. On May 11, the newspaper delivered a seventy-two-hundred-word mea culpa, though perhaps it would be better termed a "non-mea-culpa mea culpa." And similar to Lott's "non-apology apology," the *New York Times* piece did not quell the outrage. In fact, it added fuel to the fires inside and outside the paper.

In addition to **Poynter Online**, where anonymous e-mails and memos were continuing to appear, there was another neoblog making trouble for the *Times*. The online home of *Newsweek* hosted **Raw Copy**, which was where Seth Mnookin wrote and published *Times*-related articles at a clip much faster than the weekly ordinarily worked. Mnookin wrote on May 12 that "there's plenty that the *Times* report . . . didn't fully explore, namely how a troubled young reporter whose short career was rife with problems was able to advance so quickly." Meanwhile, Romenesko posted a letter from Kevin Hoffman of **Cleveland Scene** (**clevescene.com**) that stated, "What this scandal really points out is how woefully inept our industry is at preventing plagiarism and fiction from entering the public record. The real blame must be laid on the doorstep of the experienced veterans who greenlighted the work." Andrew Sullivan could not have agreed more, though his way of putting it certainly seemed more in tune with the blogosphere outcry:

> What seems obvious is that Blair wasn't that enterprising or clever; his lies were easily checked; the travel receipts he submitted were proof enough of his deception; his own editors were aware of the problems and told management; there were plenty of complaints from readers; and so on. The scandal, in other words, isn't what an overwhelmed, twenty-something young reporter succeeded in getting away with. The scandal is how he wasn't stopped, and despite crystal-clear warnings, was actually promoted at the behest of the highest authorities in the place: Gerald Boyd and Howell Raines.

The continual flow of evidence seemed to place responsibility for the fiasco on Howell Raines. On May 12, a memo titled "A Message to the Staff from Howell Raines" was leaked to Romenesko and posted on **Poynter Online**. It contained the following tidbit:

"This week I will meet individually with each member of our reporting team to hear from them, directly and unfiltered, their conclusions about these lapses and what corrective steps are needed." Also in this memo was the fact that "The Siegal Committee" had been formed to get to the bottom of what went wrong. It was already well known that Raines had ignored urgent appeals to get rid of Blair from his own editors, including the metro editor, who pleaded, "Stop Jayson from writing for the *Times*. Right Now."

That appeal had been made a year before Blair was exposed. Kaus once again found a clever way of framing the situation: "I get it: If only Raines meets with enough editors and reporters, then his high-handed dismissal of editors' and reporters' advice will be better-informed."

The result of all of this stirring of pots was an emergency meeting of all *Times* staff on May 14. Matt Drudge obtained the e-mail announcing the gathering and posted it on his website. The proceedings might as well have been broadcast on C-SPAN, for the blogosphere quickly obtained and distributed the accounts from staffers.

According to Sullivan, the meeting was "an extraordinary outpouring of anger from the staff of the *New York Times* at the mercurial, arbitrary and incompetent management of executive editor, Howell Raines." To its credit, the *Times* reported the goings-on of this meeting on its own. Most striking was Raines's admission:

> "You view me as inaccessible and arrogant," Mr. Raines said, ticking off a list he had compiled from his own newsroom interviews in recent days. "You believe the newsroom is too hierarchical, that my ideas get acted on and others get ignored.

I heard that you were convinced there's a star system that singles out my favorites for elevation." "Fear," he added, "is a problem to such extent, I was told, that editors are scared to bring me bad news."

Although nearly everyone now agreed that there were serious problems at the *Times*, not everyone had been willing to accept that the affirmative action program was specifically to blame. Mnookin himself had written the following about a May 12 *Hardball* discussion: "Liz Swasey, a mouthpiece for the benignly named Media Research Center, a right-wing attack group, smeared Howell Raines's and the *New York Times*' commitment to diversity." Mnookin went on to say that he "openly laughed" at Swasey.

During the emergency meeting, however, Raines finally settled the race issue when asked if it had anything to do with Blair's promotion: "When I look into my heart for the truth of that, the answer is yes." Understandably, L. Brent Bozell, president of the Media Research Center (that "right-wing attack group"), had some words for Mnookin and his employer *Newsweek*: "Despite Mr. Raines's admission, Mr. Mnookin's discredited piece smearing my employee remains the number two story on *Newsweek.com*. I ask that the piece be removed. I also challenge Mr. Mnookin to be man enough to apologize to Ms. Swasey." The blogosphere had thus spawned a controversy about a controversy. It would happen again, as the new journalism culture that has sprung up is accountable in ways that old journalism never has been.

Back at the *Times*, the question was now whether Raines and his number two, Gerald Boyd, would survive. Andrew Sullivan summed up why the fate of the two were tied: "Usually, the head-guy gets his underling to walk the plank, which, in this case, would be Boyd. But the *Times* can hardly be seen to fire not one but two black staffers, so Boyd stays."

Focus was also on Arthur "Pinch" Sulzberger Jr., the scion of the *Times*'s family-owned tradition. At the emergency meeting Sulzberger had said he would refuse Raines's resignation even if it were offered. The days when such an unequivocal vote of confidence could quell a revolt were over, though, and if anything Sulzberger's line in the sand upped the pressure.

The blogosphere had, by this point, opened three fronts on Howell Raines: his negligent oversight, his imperious managing style, and his preferential treatment of Blair believed by many to be rooted in Blair's race. Raines was at the point where nothing else could go wrong.

Enter Rick Bragg, another *New York Times* reporter. When examination of Bragg's reporting for the paper revealed that he had filed stories on events he did not completely witness from cities he had left, Bragg responded that "it is common for *Times* correspondents to slip in and out of cities to 'get the dateline' while relying on the work of stringers, researchers, interns and clerks." Such practices might have been common in the days before instant accountability and the demand for transparency and accuracy, but not any longer.

Jay Rosen, NYU professor of journalism and perhaps the most respected academic blogger focusing on the blogosphere, pointed out that bloggers were part of a new culture of hyper-scrutiny: "Bragg is probably kind of an arbitrary victim of that . . . For a long time journalists haven't had to explain very much how they do things . . . The internet has created the expectation that news organizations can be interacted with, can be questioned."

The new culture brought the focus, and coworkers brought the evidence. Bragg was shown, along with everyone else, what his coworkers thought of him on **Poynter Online**. Romenesko also posted an internal memo by younger *Times* reporters and a Gallup poll that showed only 36 percent of respondents trusted the media. None of these postings helped Bragg, or by extension, Raines.

During the emergency meeting, there was another episode that caught the blogosphere's attention and triggered one of its favorite devices: ridicule. "In a surreal moment that reminded one staffer of Shari Lewis' old TV show," reported the *New York Daily News*, "Sulzberger produced a stuffed toy moose that he sometimes trots out as a symbol of open communication." After displaying the moose, Sulzberger handed it to Raines. Chris Regan of **JunkYardBlog (junkyardblog.transfinitum.net)** made this observation: "Sulzberger is strategically driving the appearance of change to justify his own unwillingness to step down as the chief moose." The passing of the moose, according to Regan, was symbolic of Sulzberger's laying the blame elsewhere.

The moose triggered ridicule. Ridicule and the *Times* do not go together. The pressure within and outside of the *Times* mounted. It did not appear that there was any way to turn attention away from the paper's internal meltdown. Raines and Boyd sent yet another memo to all hands on May 29, proclaiming their confidence in the paper's integrity.

Raines and Boyd gave up and resigned a week later on June 5, 2003.

Tim Rutten of the *Los Angeles Times*—a lefty, but a fair reporter of media meltdowns—observed that "in the end, it was the new world of websites, blogs, online editions and e-mails—not Raines—that set the pace of his exit."

The blogosphere was all about speed, Kathleen Parker wrote, and it needed a new word: "'instanity' . . . news in a pixel instant because New York minutes have gotten too slow."

It was nothing personal, really; it was just that nobody liked Raines, and a new machinery to communicate that dislike had appeared just as Raines committed blunder after blunder. As with Lott, people kept lining up to beat him like a bongo drum.

One big blogging voice was generally absent from the *New York Times* scandal. Joshua Micah Marshall, who was so vociferous in his attacks on Senator Lott, mentioned the scandal at the *Times* only once, and it was embedded within a larger post defending Maureen Dowd's doctoring of a Bush quote. Glenn Reynolds even linked to Marshall and declared **Talking Points Memo** a "Blair-scandal-free zone."

What Marshall did write follows: "I'm no fan of Howell Raines, who did as much as anyone to advance the Clinton pseudo-scandals while he was editor of the *Times* Op-Ed page. Note to 'wingers: think twice before you try to ditch him, he's done a lot for you guys!" Later in the post, Marshall returned to the subject: "As I said above, I have little positive feeling for Raines . . . The Blair scandal has exposed some very serious management problems at the *Times*. And the more recent Bragg scandal-ette shows what I'd call an institutional arrogance that is at a minimum troubling."

Thus did the hyper-partisan Marshall declare his colors. He did not think that he should join the "wingers" in ditching a man as guilty as Raines. The center-right bloggers had been part of the effort to oust Lott, but the lefty hyper-partisan Marshall provided an early example that the blogosphere, like MSM, had its corners where partisan advantage would trump story line.

Raines would eventually provide his own take on what happened in a huge article for the *Atlantic Monthly*'s May 2004 issue. "I am not going to spend the rest of my life going over the details of the Blair scandal," Raines wrote. "My intention here is to perform a final service for the newspaper that I worked for and loved for twenty-five years, by revealing the real struggle that was going on behind the scenes at the *Times* as the Blair scandal played out."

Slate's Jack Shafer said of the piece that it revealed Raines to be "bitter, conceited, and clueless." Mostly, though, it revealed him to be verbose. Raines ought to have simply written: "It was the bloggers that got me." He would have been right.

CHRISTMAS-EVE-NOT-IN-CAMBODIA

And then the blogosphere rested. It was still out there, growing in influence and readership, but even though many had predicted big things for the blogs during the presidential campaign of 2004, most of that campaign had been conducted and the Democratic nominee formally crowned in Boston before the blogs made a lasting impact.

The Dean campaign might argue differently, as its use of the blogs helped organize a lot of Dean's early support into a political organization and a media phenomenon. Certainly the Deaniacs loved their blogs, but when push came to shove in Iowa, Dean melted away. The Dean Scream and not the Dean Team was the story of that campaign.

When the blogs first made their presence felt, it was as a life-support system for a story the MSM did not want to touch. With Lott and Raines the blogs had cued and then cooperated with the MSM and forced the pace of stories that were quickly adopted by the established bigs of the media world. With the assault on John Kerry's credibility as it related to his claims of cross-border adventures in Cambodia on Christmas Eve 1968, the blogs and talk radio owned the entire story in early August 2004 and forced the MSM to confront Kerry's fabrications despite the reluctance of the MSM to do so.

On *The Dick Cavett Show*, June 30, 1971, a clean-cut Navy veteran, John O'Neill, took on a hostile crowd, a condescending host, and a shaggy John Kerry, who had been spending his time since returning from Vietnam in various political endeavors, including a testimony before the Senate calling his fellow veterans war criminals and a campaign of his own for Congress. In the ensuing televised debate, O'Neill had the following to say:

> Mr. Kerry is the type of person who lives and survives only on the war weariness and fears of the American people. This is the same little man who on nationwide television in April spoke of, quote, "crimes committed on a day-to-day basis with the full awareness of officers at all levels of command," who was quoted in a prominent news magazine in May as saying, quote, "war crimes in Vietnam are the rule and not the exception," unquote. Who brought 50 veterans down to Washington to testify about alleged atrocities in April, the same 50 who after they had appeared on every major news network refused to provide any depositions or provide any details of any kind. Never in the course of human events have so many been libeled by so few.

Looking back on that debate thirty-three years later, it is clear that O'Neill got the best of the haughty and ineffective Kerry then, but the nation was growing weary of the war and its issues. O'Neill left the national stage and moved on to Texas Law School, graduated at the top of his class, clerked for Supreme Court Justice William H. Rehnquist, and became a name partner of a successful Houston law firm. He left his personal disgust of Kerry behind and let Kerry go on to do whatever he may in Massachusetts. Then, Kerry decided to run for president.

The sting of those libels uttered by Kerry during his protest career never faded. When Kerry seized the Democratic nomination in 2004, the men he had libeled thirty years earlier sprang into action.

According to their website, the Swift Boat Veterans for Truth (**www.SwiftVets.com**), the group headed by John O'Neill, was formed

> to counter the false "war crimes" charges John Kerry repeatedly made against Vietnam veterans who served in our units and elsewhere, and to accurately portray Kerry's brief tour in Vietnam as a junior grade Lieutenant . . . For more than thirty years, most Vietnam veterans kept silent as we were maligned as misfits, addicts, and baby killers. Now that a key creator of that poisonous image is seeking the Presidency we have resolved to end our silence.

John O'Neill, the thorn in Kerry's side in 1971, was officially back, and this time he wasn't alone. Scores of other Swift Boat Veterans, as well as disgusted Vietnam-era veterans and many POWs from that war, banded together to raise questions about Kerry's fitness to command America's military given his conduct and reckless charges thirty years earlier. But they had no expectation of a fair shake from the MSM, and at least initially, they received none. O'Neill's book, *Unfit for Command*, soared to the top of best-seller lists across the country, but not because of any help he received from opinion elites.

Most bloggers noted the entrance of the Swift Boat Veterans for Truth to the national stage, but nearly all expressed reservations about the effort, including me. I and most others were concerned that no "charge-countercharge" exchange on the specifics of Kerry's activities in Vietnam would ever give anyone who wasn't there any reason to conclusively consider Kerry "fit" or "unfit." Kerry had volunteered for the Swift Boats and had been highly decorated for his service. Civilians were very reluctant to enter this battle among combat veterans. This was a common reaction to news of the approach of the Swift Boat Vets.

Blackfive (Blackfive.net), a very respected milblogger (such a blogger is one who is either on active duty in the military or with extensive military service that informs his or her commentary), confessed early on, "I understand the anger directed at John Kerry by veterans—especially, Vietnam vets. I understand and share their outrage that anyone is taking this man seriously. But we must temper the anger and outrage with thoughtful discourse or we stand the chance of not being heard at all." While this post was written before the Swift Vets had banded together, it reflected the consensus position in the blogosphere to accept and honor Kerry's service, while blasting the excesses of his protest record.

BeldarBlog (www.beldar.org), another blogger, and like many of the best bloggers, a lawyer with tremendous experience, wrote a very favorable post about the character of John O'Neill, whom **Beldar** had cross-examined in a trial and had been very impressed with. He prefaced his vouching for O'Neill, however, with the following: "On the subject of Sen. Kerry's military record, I've written on my own blog and elsewhere that I don't doubt Kerry's patriotism, and that I genuinely honor his service to his country. I continue to do so."

The Swift Vets were thus in danger of being marginalized even before their campaign had begun because nobody wanted to talk about Kerry's Vietnam service. Nobody, that is, except for John

Kerry. When he gave his acceptance speech at the Democratic National Convention, he began with, "I'm John Kerry, and I'm reporting for duty."

His campaign had decided that its foundation would be Kerry's Vietnam service, not his Senate record. During the convention, a video of his service was put together by Steven Spielberg's protégé James Moll. The context of the Global War on Terror made Kerry's record as a decorated vet who had shown courage under enemy fire seem like the strongest card Kerry had to play against a wartime president, especially when the twenty years he had spent in the Senate had largely been in the service of way-left causes such as the nuclear freeze, the anti-Contra efforts, and his systematic attempts to cut weaponry and intelligence budgets.

After Kerry had made Vietnam central to his campaign, it made the criticisms of his Vietnam service potentially more pertinent to the election. The week after the Democratic National Convention, the first advertisement by the Swift Boat Veterans for Truth was released, along with O'Neill's book. While MSM raised and debated the red herring of Bush-Cheney '04 ties to the Swift Vets—these men would have run the same ads no matter whom Kerry ran against, and no matter how early and often they were urged by the president or his team to stop; it wasn't about Bush, but about Kerry—the elites never bothered to actually read what O'Neill had written. Crucially, the publisher hit upon a promotional step that would have wide-ranging effects. A sample chapter from the book was released to anyone who bothered to download it over the internet.

While reactions to the Swift Vets' approach varied, including a condemnation by Republican Senator and Vietnam veteran John McCain, in the blogosphere the reaction was quite different.

The **Instapundit**, Glenn Reynolds, wrote that "Kerry played right into this with all the stuff about Vietnam and medals." On August 5, the Kerry campaign threatened to sue stations that ran the television ad. This threat backfired, bringing the Swift Vets attention and sympathy, as **PowerLine** pointed out: "The Swift Boat Vets don't have the money to secure broad distribution for their ad. Their strategy, obviously, is to try to make up in news coverage what they lack in cash. It seems to me that Kerry's strategy plays into the Vets' hands. The more time between now and November that is spent debating the truth of the Vets' charges, the worse for John Kerry."

But the major obstacle for the Swift Vets remained: the "fog of war" that hangs over the conflicting accounts of Kerry's service could not be decisively cleared away. The Swift Vets needed a solid, indisputable news peg.

They got it in the "Christmas Eve in Cambodia in 1968" story.

The chapter from *Unfit for Command* released over the internet contained O'Neill's critique of Kerry's long record of asserting that he had been in Cambodian waters with his boat on an illegal mission on Christmas Eve 1968. There was no "he said vs. he said" dynamic at work here. All of the claims being examined first by O'Neill in his book, and then by the new media, had been made by Kerry himself.

Here is what Kerry had said on the floor of the United States Senate in 1986: "I remember what it was like to be shot at by Vietnamese and Khmer Rouge and Cambodians, and have the President of the United States telling the American people that I was not there; the troops were not in Cambodia. I have that memory which is seared—seared—in me."

It wasn't the first time Kerry had made such a claim. In an article Kerry wrote for the *Boston Herald* on October 14, 1979, he said: "I remember spending Christmas Eve of 1968 five miles across the Cambodian border being shot at by our South Vietnamese allies who were drunk and celebrating Christmas. The absurdity of almost being killed by our own allies in a country in which President Nixon claimed there were no American troops was very real."

O'Neill asserted this claim was wholly and provably false. When I read the downloaded chapter on August 5, I was broadcasting from Sacramento and had a rare live audience in front of me in addition to my audience in seventy cities across the country. The reaction of the live audience to O'Neill's charge that Kerry had invented secret missions was a very bright signal flare—they were astonished. Could any public figure be so odd as to invent secret adventures?

I could not believe that Kerry would lie about so easily disproved a matter, and I told my audience to withhold judgment, but that if Kerry had in fact made up secret missions to Cambodia, the fallout would be enormous. The *Weekly Standard*'s Jonathan Last described what happened next:

> But the big news on August 6 was that Regnery allowed people to download the "Christmas in Cambodia" section of O'Neill's book. While [Keith] Olbermann and others were worrying about mystical jazz, the new media swung into action. Hugh Hewitt, Glenn Reynolds, PowerLine, and other bloggers immediately began investigating the book's allegations. The blog JustOneMinute was the first to find the 1986 "seared—seared" speech in which Kerry described his memory of being in Cambodia in December 1968. On August 8, Reynolds took his digital camera to the University of Tennessee law library and photographed the section of the Congressional Record with

the Kerry speech, further verifying the chapter's central claim. That same weekend, Al Hunt talked about the Swift boat ad on CNN's Capital Gang, calling it "some of the sleaziest lies I've ever seen in politics."

Over the next eleven days, an interesting dynamic took hold: talk radio and the blog world covered the Cambodia story obsessively. They reported on border crossings during Vietnam and the differences between swift boats and PBRs (Patrol Boat Rivers). **Froggy Ruminations (www.froggyruminations.blogspot.com)** was launched by a former Navy SEAL, providing details on the secret war of that era, aspects that did not support Kerry's version of events. They also found two other instances of Kerry's talking about his Christmas in Cambodia. Spurred on by the blogs, FOX News led the August 9 *Special Report* with a Carl Cameron story on Kerry's Cambodia discrepancy.

All the while, traditional print and broadcast media tried hard to ignore the story—even as Kerry officially changed his position on his presence in Cambodia. Then on August 19, Kerry went public with his counterassault against Swift Boat Veterans for Truth, and suddenly the story was news. The numbers are fairly striking: before August 19, the *New York Times* and *Washington Post* had each mentioned Swift Boat Veterans for Truth just eight times; the *Los Angeles Times* seven times; the *Boston Globe* four times. The broadcast networks did far less. According to the indefatigable Media Research Center, before Kerry went public, ABC, CBS, and NBC together had done a total of nine stories on the Swifties. For comparison, as of August 19 these networks had done seventy-five stories on the accusation that Bush had been AWOL from the National Guard.

Blogger **Roger L. Simon** (RogerLSimon.com) explained why

he, along with most of the blogosphere, found the "Christmas-Eve-not-in-Cambodia" story so disturbing: "I don't like the idea of having a man who sounds like a pathetic barroom blowhard (and that's what he sounds like to me) becoming President of the United States in a time of war. People like this start to believe their own lies." Even lefty blogger Matthew Yglesias expressed some worry about the story, though he maintained it was most likely untrue at the time: "It certainly looks bad from here, and I haven't seen a good explanation yet, perhaps because there isn't one. It's a little hard to see what could possibly be the motive for a Kerry lie on this front, which makes it plausible that there's a reasonable explanation, but also a little freaky if there does not turn out to be one."

Even as bloggers exposed the various Cambodia-related lies—a tip led me to a *U.S. News & World Report* article in 2000 in which Kerry had claimed to run guns to anticommunists—another almost certain invention of Kerry's active imagination—they also kept the heat on MSM. On August 12, Glenn Reynolds began his post on the subject by noting that neither the *New York Times* nor the *Washington Post* had written about "Christmas Eve in Cambodia" "even though the Kerry Campaign has now admitted that Kerry's oft-repeated stories about being in Cambodia on Christmas Day, 1968 aren't true." I repeatedly brought attention to the fact that a *Washington Post* story had contained an anecdote from Kerry to the *Post* reporter about ferrying a CIA man into Cambodia, a story that concluded with Kerry showing the reporter the "lucky hat" that the CIA man had given Kerry. I started calling this Kerry's "magic hat," a tag I am pleased to see has resonated far and wide.

Will Collier, one of the contributors to **Vodkapundit** (**www.vodkapundit.com**), also included a roundup of media outlets that were ignoring the story; the list was extensive. A week later, the *Los Angeles Times* finally broke its silence on the Cambodia story, not surprisingly coming down on the side of Kerry, but blogger **Patterico** fisked this article thoroughly. The *Washington Post* continued to ignore the story, though Charles Austin blogged that the newspaper did run a "correction" on one of the Swift Vets' claims: "Isn't it interesting that in the case of the Swift Boat Veterans for Truth, the 'correction' appears on page one above the fold, while the original news was buried on page 19."

For its part, the *New York Times* simply ran a "hit piece" on the Swift Boat Veterans for Truth. The media refused to cover this story to a proper extent. Then, proving the media truly lived in a surreal world, Reynolds noted: "After a lengthy period of ignoring [the story], a question [from *Editor & Publisher*]: 'Campaign Journalists: Has Swift Boat Story Gone on Too Long?'"

John Cole of **Balloon Juice** (**balloon-juice.com**) did a little comparative Googling between the Bush National Guard story and the Swift Boat Veterans story and found predictable results. Other commentators, including the hardest-working of them all, **Captain's Quarters**, kept adding details and sidebars and unexpected sources. Though MSM had never covered the story, all of America that followed the presidential campaign knew about it. The MSM blockade had been broken.

The Christmas-Eve-not-in-Cambodia became shorthand for Kerry's fantasy life, and suddenly the Swift Vets had credibility— and money, as internet donations flowed into their coffers. With the foothold that this big authentication provided, other counterattacks on the MSM's dismissiveness of the Swift Vets could be mounted. Most notable among the discredited claims launched against the Swift Vets was the original charge that none of the Swift Vets served on Kerry's actual boat. This charge ran in that

Los Angeles Times article on the front page. Blogger **Patterico** demanded a correction simply because "Steven Gardner, a member of the Swift Boat Veterans for Truth, served on one of Kerry's patrol boats during the war." For the first time the MSM had to deal with a legion of genuine ombudsmen and genuine editors, not colleagues in the agenda journalism business.

Throughout the campaign many in the MSM continued to deride the Swift Vets, ubiquitously referring to their claims as "debunked" or "unsubstantiated," despite the fact that bloggers as well as the Swift Vets had proven some of their claims to be unambiguously true, most important among them the fact that Kerry had definitely and frequently exaggerated his wartime exploits, usually in the service of his politics. Had new media not been there to provide the oxygen to those stories in early August, the Swift Vets might never have been able to escape the label of "fanatics." But the new media was there, did provide the oxygen, and the Swift Vets raised awareness of many issues connected to Kerry, the most damaging of which was Kerry's record of Walter Mitty–like fables about himself.

BLOG BREAKOUT: ROUTING RATHER

The blogosphere **August**'s validation of some of the Swift Vets' charges was followed by an even bigger contribution to Campaign 2004 in September. You can summarize it in a word: Rathergate.

The now infamous *60 Minutes 2* broadcast ran on September 8, 2004, and—based primarily on memos allegedly written by Bush superior Lt. Col. Jerry Killian in 1973—the story asserted that Bush did not do his duty and had in fact disobeyed direct orders. Whether or not these charges, had they been true, would have mattered in the campaign is beside the point, because they were not true. The Killian memos were forgeries. In fact, they were bad forgeries.

Within hours of the documents' posting on the internet by CBS the day after the story ran on television, a thread had begun on **Free Republic** concerning the broadcast, and at a minute before nine that same night, **Buckhead** posted the following examination of the memos' authenticity:

> Every single one of these memos to file is in a proportionally spaced font, probably Palatino or Times New Roman. In 1972 people used typewriters for this sort of thing, and typewriters used monospaced fonts. The use of proportionally spaced fonts did not come into common use for office memos until the introduction of laser printers, word processing software, and personal computers. They were not widespread until the mid to late 90's. Before then, you needed typesetting equipment, and that wasn't used for personal memos to file. Even the Wang systems that were dominant in the mid 80's used monospaced fonts. I am saying these documents are forgeries, run through a copier for 15 generations to make them look old. This should be pursued aggressively.

"If the documents are not what we were led to believe," Rather would say later, "I'd like to break that story." Unfortunately for Rather, it had already been broken.

Blogger **PrestoPundit** (hayekcenter.org/prestopundit) provided a summary of the dynamic that took over: "Today we are getting an experience of journalism which in the past was the privilege only of those who had some specialized knowledge of the details of the story . . . Blogging technology makes anyone with specialized knowledge an effective muckraker."

Early the next morning, September 9, Scott Johnson, "The Big Trunk" of **PowerLine,** posted the now-famous "Sixty-First Minute." Fourteen updates to the original post later, the trio of bloggers at **PowerLine** were finally forced to expand the original post into separate ones. Before that, however, the original post included an ever-growing amount of specialized information, coming from readers all over the country, and nearly all of it pointing to the conclusion that the documents were forgeries. In addition to original observation by **Buckhead**, the evidence included the following: a brief course in the history and capabilities of typewriters, the accounts of former military men who had used those typewriters, a clarification on the size of paper used at the time (unlike the size of the forged memos), the inability of most typewriters to create the superscripted "th" seen in the memos, the inability of any typewriter to "kern" (i.e., fit letters together) as the letters were in the memos, the fact that standard military operating procedures would not have permitted personal memos for that subject matter, a comparative analysis of the signatures used on authentic Killian memos and the forged ones, the proportional spacing of the memos, the anachronistic inclusion of General Staudt in the memos, and so on, and so on. The sheer amount of evidence, collected in a few short hours, is beyond staggering. It is phenomenal. Mainstream media would never be the same.

The morning that I read **PowerLine's** initial entry I immediately turned to Google to locate a document expert to interview on my radio show. I found him in Farrell Shiver, a highly qualified document expert. I interviewed him on air on the ninth, and transcribed the conversation on my blog in the hope of reassuring bloggers generally that expert opinion backed them up. The next day I would publish e-mails from Professor Robert "Corky"

Cartwright at Rice University that would be widely cited as more definitive evidence that the forgeries were in fact forgeries. **INDC Journal** had found another expert in Dr. Philip Bouffard, who declared that he was 90 percent positive that the documents were faked. Dr. Joseph Newcomer posted a detailed and final exposition on why the forgeries were forgeries, and the issue became undebatable, except by kooks and Dan Rather.

But "expert" testimony wasn't really necessary after Charles Johnson of **Little Green Footballs** reproduced the memos using word-processing equipment and then managed to overlay the forgeries with his re-creation of them on his website—demonstrating to all who would look that the case was closed. The swarm kept swarming, of course, adding detail after detail of Rather and his team's incredible obtrusiveness and naïveté, and the *Washington Post*'s enormously influential Howard Kurtz signaled to MSM that it was okay to jump onto the pile, which they did, especially at the *Post*, the *New York Post*, and the *Los Angeles Times*. Rather's reputation was in ruins, and no one doubted at all that CBS had been "had," which is exactly the conclusion a *Los Angeles Times* editorial opened with, a sure signal that Rather had no allies left on the left.

PowerLine's John Hinderacker and Scott Johnson rightly appeared on the cover of *Time*, and blogging had entered the mainstream media's awareness never to leave again.

On September 10, during the height of the controversy, bloggers had been dismissed by an ex-CBS big, Jonathan Stein, as just "guys in pajamas." This attempt to sow the impression bloggers were semi-obsessed losers ranting away and venting their frustrations to other losers in a self-contained circle of fanaticism immediately backfired as the humor-obsessed bloggers embraced the term. Jim Geraghty of **KerrySpot** (**NationalReview.com/kerry/ker** ryspot.asp) coined the term *Pajamahadeen* and the incredible power of the new medium to define any story was evident. Turning an attack back on the attacker was the defining moment of episode for the blogosphere's future. Only fools will try that gambit in the years ahead, and Mr. Stein's place in the history of journalism is right up there with the fellows who served up Ruth's, Aaron's, and Bond's record-setting swings.

The truth was and remains that many bloggers had credentials and résumés far exceeding those of "journalists" who had often spent entire careers in one organization with little experience outside their own tightly managed and self-reinforcing world. In the middle of Rathergate, the blogger **Beldar**, a very experienced trial and appellate lawyer who had once in fact defended CBS before the Fifth Circuit Court of Appeals, did an extensive post on the credentials of the major bloggers on Sunday, September 12, demonstrating that MSM really didn't want to follow up this line of counterattack. (And when the *Los Angeles Times* "exposed" the **Free Republic** poster **Buckhead**, who got the ball rolling, the paper only "discovered" that he was a successful Atlanta lawyer, Harry W. MacDougald.) MSM slowly came to realize that the best bloggers had the backgrounds that made journalism degrees pale in comparison, and the better bloggers began to appear on cable as talking heads.

Each day that Dan Rather stood by the authenticity of the documents was another day of deserved abuse within the blogosphere and MSM, and eventually most people came to see Rather as Rather had seen his original adversary President Nixon, during Watergate: caught in a cover-up, desperate for an exit that never appeared. Rather hung on to his job through the controversy and the decline in ratings and hadn't yet been shown the door as of this writing, but his reputation is now forever defined by this terrible series of judgments that is known as Ra^thergate, just as Nixon's reputation will always be burdened by Watergate. Detailed studies will go on for years, with books and seminars devoted to the particulars, but there is no changing the meta-message that CBS rushed to run a story that was ridiculously and transparently a fraud because it wanted so badly to believe it wasn't.

And that the *blogosphere* exposed the fraud with breathtaking speed and finality.

THE BLOGOSPHERE ENDGAME TO CAMPAIGN 2004

Other aspects of Campaign 2004 were influenced by the blogosphere. Sinclair Broadcasting announced plans to show a documentary titled *Stolen Honor*, but had to alter its plans when lefty bloggers organized an outcry. Blogs like Jim Geraghty's **KerrySpot, PoliPundit (Polipundit.com), The Hedgehog Report (davidwissing.com),** and **RealClearPolitics (RealClearPolitics.com)** experienced enormous growth as the public swamped their servers as the election drew close. Late-breaking stories like the disclosure of Kerry's false assertion in the second presidential debate that he had met with every member of the Security Council were trumpeted on blogs like **RedState.org** even before the paper breaking the story, *The Washington Times*, posted the story on its website. **The Mystery Pollster (mysterypollster.com)** skyrocketed in popularity as he explained the torrent of polls that flooded election coverage in late October 2004.

And when the *New York Times* launched a last-minute assault on George Bush through its front-page assertions that the Bush Administration's negligence had led to the looting of Iraqi weapons, the blogosphere went into overtime to introduce alternative interpretations and crucial omitted facts. **Captain's Quarters** and **The Belmont Club** led the way in pointing to inaccuracies in the *Times'* reporting. A blog swarm helped generate a counter-storm, and John Kerry, who had embraced the *Times'* story, found himself beseiged by arguments that he was criticizing the 3rd Infantry Division and the 101st Airborne Division, both of which had passed through the site in question on the march to Baghdad.

But the biggest contribution of the blogs to George Bush's decisive 3.5 million margin in the popular vote on November 2, 2004, may have come in what it—collectively—did not do, which was to stampede the internet with bad information on the afternoon of election day that could have energized Kerry's troops while demoralizing the president's.

Early on that afternoon **Drudge** trumpeted early exit polling data that he said was favorable for Kerry. Some bloggers at **National Review** and elsewhere received the same information, and true to blogger tradition, put the info on the public shelf, even as NRO's writers wondered aloud about the reliability of the data.

For about an hour a great unease settled among the elite of the blogosphere, which traveled through them and onto hundreds of thousands of political junkies of the right who were reading every bit of text and who reacted with stunned dismay at the alarming numbers from **KerrySpot**, **The Corner**, and **Wonkette**. On the left there was much enthusiasm: It appeared as though the left had indeed out-hustled Bush-Cheney '04 and brought new voters by the millions to the cause of ousting the incumbent. **Lileks** would later speculate that the huge and energized crowds of Kerry supporters he witnessed around Minneapolis that afternoon had been energized by the "buzz" that Kerry was winning. Such is the power of good news on the hopeful.

Some bloggers said nothing and waited—including me. Karl Rove moved first to remind key information disseminators that exit polls in 2000 had been wrong, and then to force out the news that the initial sampling had been wildly skewed toward women voters. "The data was dirty," *New York Post* columnist John Podhoretz concluded on my program. Once we had the facts, we started posting. The key: a skewed sample that should have favored Kerry dramatically had in fact only given him a small lead. As I put it, the bad news had become good news.

On the day after the election, bloggers **PowerLine** and **Beldar** credited me with a steady hand and a quick move to help stem the panic, but it was really Rove & Co. blasting out the crucial information to scores of relayers that mattered, as well as the willingness of folks at **The Corner** to keep posting in the face of criticism that turned attention back to the positives already on display. (Had **The Corner** adopted a CBS-like indifference to new facts, who knows how the afternoon might have played out.) Because the president's team understood how important accurate information is to political activists by the tens of thousands manning the Get-Out-the-Vote effort, they used the blogosphere to push the key facts in an information tug-of-war that played out in the blogosphere and on radio and television until the polls closed in Hawaii. President Bush had lost the popular vote in 2000, and many GOP office holders were turned out because the networks erroneously called Florida for Gore before polls had even closed in that state, and that experience taught the president's team that bad info can skew voter behavior. They fought back with good information, and bloggers quickly disseminated it back to the voters in the trenches. Because activists of the left did not believe the real information—that the exit polling was deeply flawed—they would experience a huge disappointment later in the night when the Bush surge made its presence known.

Had the new media of talk radio and the bloggers not existed, Drudge and Kerry's backers at CBS, ABC, and other places could easily have sparked a replay of 2000's Florida effect using the "dirty data," even though many Bush supporters had learned throughout the campaign not to trust the MSM. It was a "close-run thing," but bad exit polls were defeated by good analysis inside Bush-Cheney '04 and the modern, internet-equivalent of the ancient signal fires that would pass word from hilltop to hilltop of the approach of the enemy.

No serious damage was done to the Republican GOTV effort because the internet and radio spread the word that the equivalent of a huge head-fake had been tried and had failed. The Kerry-Edwards team might have been given some energy, but the disappointment that followed later could not have been worth the few hours of cheer.

In 2006 and 2008, look for the better campaigns to formalize their connections with leading bloggers so that information passes even more quickly and securely on the all-important day of the actual voting. "Spin alley" has always been a fixture of presidential debates. Now there is a virtual press room always up and running, and Gresham's Law can be applied to it: Bad information drives out good information. Campaigns will be increasingly designed to influence the influencers on the web, not just the networks. Everyone who has influence must be treated as such, and that includes the bloggers to whom the public turns.

You should thus be persuaded that the last couple of years have been important for blogging. But it is much bigger than that. That's like saying 1517 was a big year for Martin Luther. Both statements are true but do not communicate the scope of the change that was initiated in those years. To get a glimpse of what is coming, try examining what followed Luther's challenge to the authority of Rome. As Luther was to Leo, so bloggers are to MSM, and Luther's impact wasn't limited to the Vatican.

THE FIRST REFORMATION AND THE INFORMATION REFORMATION

Why a discussion of the Protestant Reformation in a book on blogging? The short answer: because the sixteenth and twenty-first centuries share a dramatic element in common—the birth of a revolution in communication technology. The cultural, political, and economic transformations that emerged out of the Reformation and have affected the course of Western civilization ever since were fueled in large part by the advent of an extraordinary device: the movable-type printing press.

The ability to publish books inexpensively decentralized the power of knowledge and forever changed the structure of society. Affordable reading took the role of authoritative interpretation out of the hands of the elite and allowed members of the burgeoning middle class to consider information for themselves. Ideas could circulate outside the control of the established hierarchies, allowing for new perspectives, innovation, and far greater personal freedom. Gutenberg's gift of the printed page was an invitation to new understanding and human liberty. (It also bestowed upon its recipients new responsibility for critical reflection.) As we set our feet firmly in the Information Age, an examination of the sixteenth century allows us to see how the power of publishing can change the world.

The story actually begins in AD 410. That was the year Alaric—a barbarian general—sacked Rome. Though he was unable to hold the city, the handwriting was on the wall of history. And with the final collapse of the Empire in 476, Western Europe fell backward in time for nearly a millennium. Without civil authority to maintain the peace, travel and trade quickly disintegrated. Economies collapsed, whole cultures fell—it was the Dark Ages. Indeed, the world in which Jesus grew up was vastly more advanced than that of the average European in the eleventh century.

Through the thousand years of the medieval period, the solitary institution that endured was the Roman Catholic Church. Standing above the feudal struggles of the day, the Church became guardian of Western culture. It was through the clerics and scholars of the Middle Ages that the art, music, literature, and wisdom of the classical period were preserved for future generations. And for this we have every reason to be grateful. But . . .

Earthly strength has a sinister side. While serving as the lone bastion of civility in an uncivilized world, the Church also gained unprecedented wealth and authority. By the thirteenth century, the pope had become an international head of state, wielding exceptional political, economic, and military might. The papacy also held the highest power of all—the keys to both heaven and hell, exerted in the sacrament of baptism and the threat of excommunication. This power was assured in large part by the strict control of the Church over information, particularly the interpretation of Scripture.

In the fourth century, the great biblical scholar Saint Jerome completed his translation of the original Hebrew and Greek manuscripts of the Bible into Latin (the translation is known as the Vulgate), the official language of the Roman Church. After the fall of the Roman Empire, Latin lost its place as the common language of Europe and became the sole property of the educated class—educated by the Church. For the next eleven centuries the Bible was produced exclusively in Latin, and manuscripts were available only to those for whom the Church commissioned copies to be reproduced by hand. Without access to the sacred texts, the average citizen had no ability to challenge the authorities of the day. Then as now, information is an essential element of freedom.

As early as the fourteenth century, both within and without the hierarchical structures of the Church, people were calling for reform. Priests and laity alike challenged the unchecked power of the papacy, and there were repeated calls for the Church to divest itself of worldly wealth. In turn, the response of the ecclesiastical authorities was often severe. John Wycliffe, a professor at Oxford, was condemned in 1382 for his work to translate the Bible into English. And in 1415 the Czech John Huss, deeply influenced by Wycliffe, was burned at the stake for his challenges to the pope's monarchic rule. Throughout Europe the stage was being set for the Reformation. What was lacking was critical mass. Individual reformers had the power to inspire small, local communities, but without the ability to communicate on a meaningful scale with the larger world, the momentum of reform movements was easily crushed by the powers of the day.

The balance finally began to tip in 1449. It was then that Johannes Gutenberg, a goldsmith and gem cutter by trade, was putting the finishing touches on his new invention, the world's first printing press with movable type. While it is commonly understood that the art of printing and the use of presses had been around in Europe for centuries (and movable type practiced in China centuries before), Gutenberg's mass-media machine's claim to originality was based on its unique use of a series of blocks, each bearing a single letter on its face. His first type was cast of the metals lead, antimony, and tin and consisted of 290 separate symbols. He also had to develop an ink that would not fade or be too thick. He came up with the combination of boiled linseed oil and soot. That first press was adapted from one that farmers commonly used to press grapes or olives. It was fitted with a rolling tray that enabled careful placement of damp paper and its removal after the imprint was made, a slow process by today's standards but a tremendous improvement from the tedious process of handwritten manuscripts. Gutenberg's first book took fully two years to produce, and it was: the Vulgate.

With the advent of movable type, the average cost of a book fell roughly 400 times. Soon intellectual life was no longer the exclusive domain of church and court, and literacy became a necessity of urban existence. The printing press stoked intellectual fires at the end of the Middle Ages, helping usher in an era of enlightenment. This great cultural rebirth was inspired by widespread access to and appreciation for classical art and literature, and these translated into a renewed passion for artistic expression. Without the development of the printing press, the Renaissance would never have happened. Without inexpensive printing to make books available to a large portion of society, any number of writers, musicians, politicians, clergy, scientists, physicians, and explorers would not have had a way to relay their knowledge and inspiration. Without access to the thoughts of others, the Reformers of the sixteenth century could never have changed the world.

Martin Luther, the Father of the Reformation, was born to an essentially middle-class family in Saxony in 1483. His father was a miner who, having achieved some level of prosperity, desperately wanted his son to pursue a career in the law—a desire Martin intended to honor. Luther earned his undergraduate degree from the University of Erfurt in 1505, planning to enter law school in September of that same year. In July, while out for a summer walk in the forest, Luther was caught in a violent thunderstorm and nearly struck by lightning. Overcome by fear, he offered fervent prayers to Saint Anne (the patron saint of miners, and pregnant women; he was probably thinking in terms of the former), vowing to enter the monastery if he survived. Less than a month later he joined the Augustinian Order in Erfurt.

Throughout his life, Luther was a man of strong emotion, given to depression and troubled by self-doubt. Both his parents were devout Catholics, and Luther was raised in an atmosphere of severity and piety. His mother was particularly strict, and Luther is known to have struggled even in his early years with guilt and the inescapable fear of the judgment of Christ. By temperament he was not drawn to monastic life, but he desperately desired to serve God and looked upon his experience in the forest as part of the divine plan. He took his ordination vows to the priesthood in 1507, with a certain idealism about his devotion to the Church.

In the years that followed, Luther became ever more disillusioned with Catholicism. His monastery was strict in its devotion, but Luther imposed an even stricter self-discipline upon himself in an effort to rid his conscience of guilt. He spent countless hours in prayer and vigils, fasted for days on end—more than once to the point of fainting—but to no avail. Indeed, his efforts in confession were the source of mockery among the other monks (they used to say that he went to confession every time he suffered from gas). In 1510 his supervisor sent him on a trip to Rome in the hopes of loosening him up, but the experience proved only more disheartening. It was in Rome that Luther first came face-to-face with the laxity and corruption that were deeply rooted within the Church, and he returned home more despairing than he'd left.

At the heart of Luther's internal struggle was his sense of a deep need for forgiveness. It was the teaching of the Church that reparation for sin was made by confession and penance (a punishment imposed by the Church as the temporal consequence of sin). But no matter how fervent Luther's devotion, how exact his penance, he could find no inner solace.

In 1511 Luther accepted a professorial position at the University of Wittenberg, where he found substantial professional success; but peace of mind continued to elude him. It came somewhere between 1513 and 1517. Though he had certainly studied them before, the time was now ripe and he was, for the first time, struck by the words of the apostle Paul in his letter to the Roman church: "Now it is evident that no one is justified before God by the law; for 'The one who is righteous will live by faith'" (Galatians 3:11). These words had an immediate and transformational impact on Luther. At once he grasped what had been lost on many in the Church for centuries—the biblical conception of grace. Sinners are not justified by piety, sincerity of confession, allegiance to the Church, or penitential obedience, but by faith in Christ. From that moment forward, justification by faith became the heart of Luther's understanding of the gospel, and later the central theological theme of the Reformation.

Luther's new appreciation of grace led him in turn to question all that he had previously embraced of Church tradition, in particular the Church's interpretation of, and stranglehold upon,

Scripture. He quickly came to believe that God intended to establish relationships with individual Christians, each capable of approaching God in Christ without the need for a priestly mediator. Consequently, the papal office was not God's provision of a vicarious presence of Christ on earth, but a corruption of the Church. Scripture was not the private property of the ecclesiastical elite, but the revelation of God for every human. From these conclusions emerged the great confessions of the Reformation:

Sola Scriptura:	By Scripture Alone
Sola Gratia:	By Grace Alone
Solus Christus:	By Christ Alone
Sola Fide:	By Faith Alone
Sola Deo Gloria:	Glory to God Alone

Luther's break with Rome became imminent in 1517, the year of his famed Ninety-five Theses. It is no small irony that Luther's last straw was itself the product of the printing press: the sale of indulgences.

According to the Catholic teaching of the medieval period, Christ's atoning death on the cross was such an expression of forgiveness—above and beyond redeeming the sins of the world—as to leave a bit left over for disbursement at the hand of the Church. This "treasury of merits" was made available for purchase to everyone from kings to paupers as a substitute first for penance, and later in lieu of actual repentance. As the name implies, an indulgence allowed the owner to escape the temporal or even eternal consequences of sin, and in turn it filled the treasury of the pope. (We can at least take heart in knowing that indulgences were often sold on a sliding scale. Historian E. G. Schwieber reports that in Luther's day the standard cost was twenty-five gulden for a king or archbishop, down to a mere half-gulden for the poor, and free to the destitute.)

In 1513 the Archbishop of Mainz (a position of strong ecclesiastical power in Germany) died. At this time in history, such a title assured a sizable income and it was therefore expected that the new appointee would pay a fee to the Church as a matter of his installation to office, often supplementing the fee with an additional "donation." In other words, then as now, money talks, and positions of power within the Church were often sold to the highest bidder. In this case the highest bidder was Albert of Mainz, who paid more than double the expected fee—an exceptionally large sum. This debt was financed by a loan from the House of Fugger, who accepted as collateral a papal bull from Pope Leo X allowing for the sale of indulgences throughout much of Germany. Schwieber notes that the bull was worded so broadly that the purchaser would receive complete absolution, with very few exceptions, from even the greatest sins upon the instant of confession, essentially binding the priest hearing confession from requiring penance or even repentance on the part of one holding the letter of indulgence. The funds raised with these indulgences would be used to repay the debt of Albert and to contribute to the construction of Saint Peter's in Rome.

The man retained by Albert to sell indulgences in the area of Wittenberg was John Tetzel, a Dominican monk with a high tolerance for personal moral ambiguity. He was known for both his brilliance of speech and his willingness to resort to threats in order to make a sale. Indeed, it seems that a favorite tactic of his was to build a fire in the town square and announce that in addition to being a seller of indulgences, he was also a hunter of heretics (remember John Huss!). He was a persuasive salesman and profits soared.

It was not long before members of Luther's congregation in Wittenberg began to arrive for confession producing their letters of indulgence to demonstrate that they were without need for further repentance. Luther was appalled. And by 1517 he was preaching and teaching boldly against Tetzel's promises of indulgence-based absolution, fearing that such spiritual laxity was leading many away from true faith in Christ.

In October of that same year, Luther decided it was time to call the other professors of the university together for a serious discussion of his concerns. To that end, he drafted his Ninety-five Theses—spelling out the issues he desired to debate. The theses were written in Latin, ensuring that they would be accessible only to scholars. And the same night (October 31) he posted them on the outside door at Castle Church in Wittenberg (the traditional manner of opening a discussion), and he sent a copy to Albert, in order to alert him to Tetzel's activities. In short, Luther made every effort to communicate through the proper channels of his day.

But Luther was living in a new day. Almost immediately after they were posted, someone, no one knows exactly who, got hold of a copy of Luther's theses, translated the Latin into German, and published them. Thanks to Gutenberg, Luther—and more important, his ideas—were known all over Germany within two weeks, and all over Europe in a month. Copies of his theses were circulating everywhere, being forwarded from friend to friend. Luther had what Wycliffe and Huss did not: technology. As Bernd Moeller put it, "Without printing, no Reformation." It took Luther from obscurity to household name nearly overnight. And his challenges to the abuses of the Church were finding resonance throughout Christendom. Needless to say, Tetzel in particular, and the Church in general, were outraged at Luther's audacity, and there were immediate calls to silence him. Luther, however, had discovered the power of the press, literally the printing press, and there was now no stopping him. Luther had been a "nobody." In an instant, he was driving history itself.

Outside the auspices of the Church, Luther began to publish in German. He took his message to the people, authoring numerous pamphlets and tracts. In his book on the subject, *Printing, Propaganda, and Martin Luther*, Mark Edwards notes that the beauty of this form was its simplicity. Many of Luther's works were in what is known as "quarto" format—four sheets of paper folded to produce eight pages. There were no covers and little or no artwork, thus allowing production to flow easily, quickly, and inexpensively (the average cost would have been about the same as one-third of a day's wages for a laborer). Their size also allowed for easy transportation and concealment, by peddlers or readers, should one be confronted by Church authorities. Edwards writes, "They were ideal for circulating a subversive message right under the noses of the opponents of reform."

Between 1517 and 1520, Luther alone authored roughly thirty works, and scholars estimate he sold more than three hundred thousand copies. And the numbers only escalated from there. Edwards reports that the period of 1517 to 1524 saw an overall fortyfold rise in the number of pamphlets published, over 6.6 million in all, the vast majority the works of the Reformers.

Edwards also notes that equally important to the number of works published was their use of the vernacular. This same period saw a dramatic reversal in the use of German over and against Latin. In 1519, for every three works in Latin, there was one published in German. By 1521, the numbers were exactly the opposite: one in Latin for every three in German. The Reformers were taking their message to the street, offering it in a simple format, accessible in both language and cost to the European "everyman."

But publishing had yet to accomplish its greatest feat of the Reformation.

In 1521 Luther began what Wycliffe had attempted more than a century prior: a translation of the Bible into the common language of the people. After all, Luther's purpose had not been to overthrow the power of the Roman Church per se. Insofar as the corruption of the Church had distorted the message of Scripture, it needed to be opposed, and passionately so. But the only way to truly reestablish a biblical faith was to restore the Bible itself to the people of God. It was only by having access to the holy texts that the average Christian could come to the same inner assurance of God's love and forgiveness that Luther himself had so powerfully experienced.

Working directly from the Greek and Hebrew originals, Luther completed a first version of his translation of the New Testament less than a year later and published a complete Bible in German in 1534. Since then, in whole or in part, the Bible has been translated into at least 2,197 languages. (And as proof that even in our accelerated culture there are still people with too much time on their hands, the Bible is currently being translated into Klingon.) It was the first printed book and perhaps the first electronic book. According to the public-domain software archive known as the PC-SIG Library, a transcription of the entire King James Bible was one of the earliest items circulated as what is called "shareware." And in September of 2004, **BibleGateway**'s website indicated that it has eighty-nine Bibles in forty-one languages now available online. Until his death in 1546, Luther was unceasing in his efforts to make the text of Scripture more available to the laity. One historian of the Reformation, Carter Lindberg, describes the passion of Luther's efforts—continually revising his translation and adding explanatory prefaces. He even intended a large-print edition for those with poor eyesight. For him, nothing could substitute for direct access to the Word of God, and he did everything within his power to make it available to everyone.

In the decades that followed, a second generation of Reformers carried Luther's reforms (and, in particular, his concern for the publication of the Bible in the common language) throughout western Europe. Most notable among them was John Calvin, born in France in 1509. He became a driving intellectual force of the Reformation, constructing the first systematic theology of the Protestant movement. His *Institutes of the Christian Religion* (first published in Latin in 1536) began as a short instructional work on the interpretation of Scripture. It was quickly revised in French and continually expanded through 1559. Almost immediately it became the primary instructional text in Protestant thought for both laity and clergy alike, further reinforcing the unique authority of the Bible in the life of the believer.

In addition, Calvin's work (like Luther's) had significant political overtones. His reflection on Rome's abuse of ecclesiastical power, his awareness of the supreme value of each individual believer to God, and his desire to faithfully enact the teaching of Scripture gave rise to a much more egalitarian form of Church government. In Geneva, where he was the head pastor from 1541 until his death in 1564, he abolished the Catholic Episcopal structure, arguing that the Bible never intended to establish a hierarchy within the Church and requiring instead that both pastors and elders (lay leaders) should be installed in office by election of the congregation they serve.

Calvin's influence had an extraordinary geographic reach, forever affecting not only the Church, but the governments of

Europe and eventually North America. And while it would be overreaching to say that the political and economic transformations that marked the beginning of the modern era were the direct result of Reformation, the latter clearly made the former possible. Luther's democratization of the Bible led, through Calvin, to the democratization of the Church. And from there, it was only a matter of time until democracy came to civil politics.

What made it all possible? What gave Luther the ability to succeed in his reform where others had failed? What allowed Calvin to shape the thought of every generation that followed him? Print. In 1449 Gutenberg amplified the human voice such that it could be heard around the world. He provided the means by which one person could communicate with the masses without the interference of the institutional structures of the day. At last individuals could speak, and none could silence them.

For the MSM, it is 1449 and 1517, at the same moment.

3

A BRIEF HISTORY OF "TEXT"

There is no doubt that the tectonic plates of journalism are moving. There is awesome potential in the internet as a gatherer, distributor and checker of news—not least through instant delivery channels such as mobile phones. This does not mean old media will die. But it will have to adapt quickly to what has so far been an asymmetrical relationship.

—Columnist Victor Keegan
of England's *The Guardian*,
September 22, 2004

When I recently decided to take a long break from blogging, it was for a mix of personal and philosophical reasons. But the direction the blogosphere is going makes me wonder whether I'll ever go back. Even as it collectively achieves celebrity status for its anti-establishment views, blogging is already being domesticated by its success. What began as a spontaneous eruption of populist creativity is on the verge of being absorbed by the media-industrial complex it claims to despise. In the process, a charmed circle of bloggers—those glib enough and ideologically safe enough to fit within the conventional media punditocracy—is gaining larger audiences and greater influence. But the passion and energy that made blogging such a potent alternative to the corporate-owned media are in danger of being lost, or driven back to the outer fringes of the internet.

—Billmon, www.billmon.com

The Los Angeles Times,

September 26, 2004

The internet has empowered ordinary citizens to become fact checkers and analysts. People with a wide range of experiences can collaborate online, sharing knowledge, sources and ideas, and challenging each others' facts.

Memogate illustrates the contrast between old media, what some call legacy media, which are built on trusting professionals to hand down the truth, and the new medium, the blogosphere, which is based on amateur journalists talking to each other. As some bloggers put it: Microsoft is old media. Linux is new media.

—Joanne Jacobs,

blogger and retired San Jose Mercury News reporter,

in a column run in the *San Francisco Chronicle*

and *St. Louis Post-Dispatch* on September 26, 2004

A year ago, no one other than campaign staffs and chronic insomniacs read political blogs. In the late 90's, about the only places online to write about politics were message boards like Salon's Table Talk or Free Republic, a conservative chat room. Crude looking weblogs, or blogs, cropped up online, and Silicon Valley techies put them to use, discussing arcane software problems with colleagues, tossing in the occasional diaristic riff on the birth of a daughter or a trip to Maui. Then in 1999, Mickey Kaus, a veteran magazine journalist and author of a weighty book on welfare reform, began a political blog on Slate. On Kausfiles, as he called it, he wrote differently ...

The Dean phenomenon drew so many new people to the grass roots (or "netroots," as the Dean bloggers used to call them) of presidential politics that a kind of fragmentation occurred in what had been, until then, a blog culture dominated by credentialed gentlemen like Kaus, Andrew Sullivan and Glenn Reynolds, a conservative law professor whose blog, Instapundit, is read faithfully at the White House.

But just as FOX News has been creaming CNN, the traffic on Kaus's and Sullivan's sites has flat-lined recently, while Atrios's and Moulitsas's are booming. Left-wing politics are thriving on blogs the way Rush Limbaugh has dominated talk radio, and in the last six months, the angrier, nastier partisan blogs have been growing the fastest. Daily Kos has tripled in traffic since June. Josh Marshall's site has quadrupled in the last year. It's almost as though, in a time of great national discord, you don't want to know both sides of an issue. The once-soothing voice of the nonideological press has become, to many readers, a secondary concern, a luxury, even something suspect. It's hard to listen to a calm and rational debate when the building is burning and your pants are smoking.

—from Matthew Klam,
"Fear and Laptops on the Campaign Trail,"
the *New York Times Magazine*,
September 26, 2004

These four quotes are drawn from old media, and from very reputable old media at that, in both the United States and in the United Kingdom. They all appeared in the aftermath of Ra^{th}ergate, a sudden, collective recognition that the old media monopoly had been shattered. A white flag of sorts, flown from West Coast to East and across the Atlantic.

Each writer had a different take, and none of them mattered. The big bang of the blogosphere may have begun just prior to **Kausfiles**'s appearance, or somewhere else along the way. But as the blogosphere hurtled out in its expanding and energizing explosion of text, it was going to follow a pattern that had been seen before. New technologies in the communication of information bring about radical change in existing hierarchies of power, and it is never pleasant for those at the top, as the Vatican discovered when Luther got his dander up.

When did the blogosphere begin? The best answer is with ancient priests of Sumer—now southern Iraq—around 3000 BC. They invented "text," in that the symbols they scratched onto clay tablets with a stylus were the first known use of writings. The Egyptians came along with hieroglyphs. Both systems were hard to use and took lifetimes to master, giving enormous authority and power to the practitioners of the craft.

Eventually mankind got around to alphabets. Perhaps the Phoenicians got the alphabet to Greece, or perhaps it got there some other way, but eventually someone wrote down *The Iliad*, and a Brad Pitt movie was under way. The Jews also had their Book, and it moved around the world with God's people. The Chinese invented paper, the Romans invented bureaucracy, and by the time of Caesar the orders, commands, accounts, and everything else that could be written down was being written down. The Church took up its place of power. Monasteries followed. When the barbarians swept over everything, the monks kept copying and the written word of mankind was preserved. As the last chapter detailed, Johannes Gutenberg opened up the doors, and publishing for the masses was under way.

But as **Lileks** would say: It. Was. All. Text.

Electricity gave the distribution of text a new velocity. Samuel Morse patented the telegraph in 1837. In 1844, Morse cabled, "What hath God wrought!" The answer: a mass market for news. Everyone wanted news, and not just around-the-corner news; they wanted "Extra! Extra! Read all about it!" news. Especially during the Civil War, and thereafter, during all wars. Morse's American Telegraph Company gave way to Western Union, which was trumped by American Telephone and Telegraph. Newspapers got their acts together, developed "professional" standards, agreed on some things, competed fiercely on others. From the online history of the Associated Press:

> On an early morning in May 1848, 10 men representing six New York City newspapers sat around an office table of the *New York Sun*. They had been in session for more than an hour and all that time they had been in stubborn argument.
>
> At issue was the costly collection of news by telegraphy. The newly invented telegraph made transmission of news possible by wire but at costs so high that the resources of any single paper would be strained.
>
> David Hale of the *Journal of Commerce* argued that only a joint effort between New York's papers could make telegraphy affordable and effectively prevent telegraph companies from interfering in the newsgathering process. To get news from the west and from abroad, Hale argued, newspapers had to work together if the public was to be served with increasingly wider coverage of the United States and the world.
>
> Although reluctant at first, the six highly competitive papers agreed to the historic plan, and The Associated Press was born.

Today, that six-newspaper cooperative is an organization serving more than 1,500 newspapers and 5,000 broadcast outlets in the United States. Abroad, AP services are printed and broadcast in 112 countries.

Worldwide, the AP serves more than 15,000 news organizations.

All fifteen thousand of those news organizations are text distributors.

Electronic news organizations are text readers. Brokaw, Jennings, and Rather are text readers. Everything that is read or orated can be transcribed to text and these days usually is. For the years from the launch of KDKA, the first commercial radio station in 1920, through to the birth and explosion of the internet, broadcasting via television or radio came to dominate the distribution of news.

From that launch in 1922, commercial radio in the United States entered an era of explosive growth as now the news could be communicated instantly and as national programming created national audiences. NBC was launched in 1926 as a partnership of RCA, GE, and Westinghouse and would later be split into NBC and ABC as a result of antitrust laws. CBS got under way as United Independent Broadcasters in 1927 but was taken over and rechristened as Columbia Broadcasting Company in 1928 by William Paley. By the time of the Depression, two of every three homes had a radio set, and FDR had begun to exploit the new medium. World War II was a radio story for most Americans, supplemented by newsreels. The election night broadcasts of 1944 were estimated to have been listened to by half of America's radio sets.

Paley had committed CBS to television in the late thirties and

BLOG

stuck with the plan to grow the new medium into the dominant broadcast vehicle. Even though 94 percent of all American households—40 million in all—owned radio sets, television quickly moved to the center of American information distribution, and the network newscasts emerged as the most important information source in America. Newspaper circulation peaked in the mid-1960s as television dominated a decade that ended with nine of ten American homes equipped with a small screen.

There were still hundreds of papers and radio stations, but the nightly news is what made the news' weather, and the American culture was shaped in large part by the content of the television programs it watched and the messages those programs delivered.

But beneath all the airtime was still text, whether teleprompter news or scripts for *Lucy*, *Laugh-In*, or *LA Law*. The relatively small number of people who composed those texts, and the texts of newspaper columns and radio copy, were the people who drove the world. They numbered in the tens of thousands, but they were still a very small percentage of America, and their elite a much smaller percentage still.

Their position on top of the information superstructure would be threatened, then undermined, and ultimately toppled by the development of the internet. There are plenty of histories of the internet available, not surprisingly, on the internet. A visionary scientist by the name of Robert Kahn is generally credited with getting the ball rolling with the research that would lead to something called ARPANET, which would in turn lead to a bewildering array of acronyms and eventually to the system we call "the internet." Says one of the many accounts available at the Internet Society's official history (**www.isoc.org/internet/history/**):

Thus, by 1985, the internet was already well established as a technology supporting a broad community of researchers and developers, and was beginning to be used by other communities for daily computer communications. Electronic mail was being used broadly across several communities, often with different systems, but interconnection between different mail systems was demonstrating the utility of broad based electronic communications between people.

The information barons didn't know it, but under their noses had been built the most revolutionary of all transmission technologies by which text could travel: easy to use, nearly cost-free, and with no control on entry or dissemination. The tools for the rise of the blogosphere were in place.

It was almost fifteen years before individuals began turning static websites into frequently updated scorecards of commentary and events and providing links there to other sites and breaking stories. A "weblog" is believed to have been first so denominated by a Jorn Barger in December of 1997. Barger's site, **Robot Wisdom.com**, is still up and going, though he's an iconoclast's iconoclast.

A trio of blogging pioneers began to count the number of weblogs in existence as 1999 began—Jesse James Garrett, Cameron Barrett, and Peter Merholz, working at **www.jjg.net/ infosift, camworld.com**, and **peterme.com** respectively—and the list wasn't long, but the attractiveness of the form became apparent to many entrepreneurs who quickly made available the "build-your-own-weblog" technology that has continued to multiply on the internet.

What happened next is best described by a press release from

Perseus Development Corporation, famous for its title: "The Blogging Iceberg":

The Blogging Iceberg: Of 4.12 Million Weblogs, Most Little Seen and Quickly Abandoned

Cambridge, MA (October 4, 2003)—For the BloggerCon 2003 conference at the Berkman Center of Harvard Law School, Perseus Development Corp. randomly surveyed 3,634 blogs (frequent publications of personal thoughts and Web links, also known as weblogs) on eight leading blog-hosting services to develop a model of blog populations. Based on this research, Perseus estimates that 4.12 million blogs have been created on these services: Blog-City, BlogSpot, Diaryland, LiveJournal, Pitas, TypePad, Weblogger and Xanga.

Based on the rapid growth rate demonstrated by the leading services, Perseus expects the number of hosted blogs created to exceed five million by the end of 2003 and to exceed ten million by the end of 2004.

ABANDONED BLOGS

The most dramatic finding from the survey was that 66.0% of surveyed blogs had not been updated in two months, representing 2.72 million blogs that have been either permanently or temporarily abandoned. "Apparently the blog-hosting services have made it so easy to create a blog that many tire-kickers feel no commitment to continuing the blog they initiate," said Jeffrey Henning, CTO of Perseus Development Corp. and author of the survey. "In fact, 1.09 million blogs were one-day wonders, with no postings on subsequent days." The average duration of the remaining 1.63 million abandoned blogs was 126 days (almost four months). A surprising 132,000 blogs were abandoned after being maintained a year or more (the oldest abandoned blog surveyed had been maintained for 923 days).

According to Perseus' survey, males were more likely than females to abandon blogs, with 46.4% of abandoned blogs created by males, as compared to 40.7% of active blogs being created by males. Abandonment rates did not vary based on age. Those who abandoned blogs tended to write posts that were only 58% as long as the posts of those who still maintained blogs, which simply indicates that those who enjoy writing stick with blogs longer.

The abandonment rate did vary significantly based on which service was being used: Pitas, BlogSpot and Diaryland had above average abandonment rates; Xanga had an average abandonment rate; LiveJournal had the lowest abandonment rate (the sample size for Blog-City, TypePad and Weblogger was too low to compare).

ACTIVE BLOGS

Blogs are famed for their linkages, and while 80.8% of active blogs linked to at least one external site from a post on their home page, these links were rarely to traditional news sources. Blogs are updated much less often than generally thought. Active blogs were updated on average every 14 days. Only 106,579 of the hosted blogs were updated on average at least once a week. Fewer than 50,000 were updated daily.

DEMOGRAPHICS

Interestingly, even as MP3 sharing and instant messaging began with teenagers, teenagers have created the majority of blogs. Blogs are currently the province of the young, with 92.4% of blogs created by people under the age of 30.

Females are slightly more likely than males to create blogs, accounting for 56.0% of hosted blogs.

According to the survey, the typical blog is written by a teenage girl who uses it twice a month to update her friends and classmates on happenings in her life. It is written very informally with slang spellings, yet not as informally as instant-messaging conversations (which are riddled with typos and abbreviations).

For more information on Perseus's survey, please contact Martha Popoloski at mpopoloski@perseus.com, Tel: 781-837-1555, or view the results online at http://www.perseus.com/blogsurvey/.

From two dozen or so blogs in early 1999 to a blogging "iceberg" of 4.12 million blogs in five years: an astonishing and still-not-quite-comprehended explosion of text greater than any in the history of humankind. So what if most of the words typed were unread. It is the explosion that mattered, not its early shape. Text producers for a mass audience have gone from a handful of ancient priests, through Gutenberg and his followers, through Morse, then Paley, and a thousand editors to everyone and anyone with access to a computer.

Perseus's finding that "fewer than 50,000 [of the millions of blogs] were updated daily" was the sleeper fact in the Perseus presentation. From the big bang of blogging, fifty thousand new virtual newspapers had been born, for that's what an "updated daily" blog is: a newspaper with one editor and as many sources as he or she cares to link to. The power of elites to determine what was news via a tightly controlled dissemination system was shattered. The ability and authority to distribute text are now truly democratized.

The audience for information has always been there. The struggle to control information flow, and the profits and power that go with that control, started in Sumer five thousand years ago. Now that struggle is effectively over. Anyone who wants a say can have it, though attention to that "say" must be earned.

Anyone who wants attention or publicity can work for it, though it may not come. The playing field is hardly level, as old elites in MSM still have extraordinary inherited advantages, as do all aristocracies entering a revolutionary epoch.

From 1983 to 2003, critics of MSM from the left pointed to the huge concentration of media outlets in fewer and fewer corporate hands. One graph expressed this concern by charting the number of corporations that controlled a majority of U.S. media outlets, including radio stations, magazines, publishing houses, television networks, etc. This chart, found at **www.corporations.org/media/media-ownership.gif**, put the number of corporations holding 50 percent or more of these assets at fifty in 1983, but only five in 2004. The concern from the left: All news would favor corporate advantage.

From the right came the well-known refrain of endemic and increasingly obvious left-tilting media bias.

The rise of the blogosphere is an answer to both complaints. Not yet a complete answer, but the beginning of the solution to all of the problems associated with a scarcity of outlets for text.

Now, even though the playing field isn't even, at least the gates are open to anyone who wants a game. The effects have been immediate.

PART II

WHAT IS HAPPENING RIGHT NOW, AND WHY

4

THERE IS A NEW
SHERIFF IN TOWN

Actually, there are a million new sheriffs in town.

As Rathergate crescendoed to its conclusion, a writer named Ben Wasserstein took to the pages of the Sunday opinion section of the *Los Angeles Times* on September 19, 2004, and under the title "Bloggers' 'Moment' Doesn't Make a Revolution," he tried to claim the world was flat. About the toppling of Rather, Wasserstein wrote that "bloggers cheered that the new media David had slain the old media Goliath," and that "right-wing bloggers have tasted blood—and they like it. Best of all it was CBS News, Rather and '60 Minutes,' three bastions of establishment journalism, reaping the whirlwind."

And then Wasserstein spent about eighteen column inches explaining why it was really no big deal, why old media is still the dominant force, and why the "blogs picked up the story, but they couldn't carry it to the finish line alone. They were complemented by traditional media, but never came close to supplanting it."

A classic Black Knight moment. The Black Knight is a character from *Monty Python and the Holy Grail*, who, even as he is dismembered stroke by stroke, continues to proclaim loudly his invincibility. Mr. Wasserstein boldly charged out into the editorial section of one of the old media giants to proclaim to the bloggers: "You Shall Not Pass!" Had the bloggers bothered to notice Mr. Wasserstein, he'd have been left as immobile as the Black Knight, but they barely paused. There was a presidential race to cover and a war in Iraq to analyze.

Similarly, the day after Wasserstein dismissed the effectiveness of the blogs, *Time* magazine put out a cover story on Rathergate, complete with a story on the blogs' role, and a commentary by one of the bigger bloggers, Andrew Sullivan, who wrote in part:

> Does this mean the old media is dead? Not at all. Blogs depend on the journalistic resources of big media to do the bulk of reporting and analysis. What blogs do is provide the best scrutiny of big media imaginable—ratcheting up the standards of the professionals, adding new voices, new perspectives and new facts every minute. The genius lies not so much in the bloggers themselves but in the transparent system they have created. In an era of polarized debate, the truth has never been more available. Thank the guys in the pajamas. And read them.

On the day this issue of *Time* appeared, I checked the ranking of blogs in terms of popularity by visitors, maintained by a site named **The Truth Laid Bear** (**truthlaidbear.com**) maintained by **N. Z. Bear**. Here's where the traffic flowed on September 20, 2004:

WEBLOGS BY AVERAGE DAILY TRAFFIC

Traffic statistics via
SiteMeter
Ecosystem ranking is provided in ( )

1) Instapundit.com 300543 visits/day (1)

2) Daily Kos 267202 visits/day (3)

3) Eschaton 147088 visits/day (5)

4) Gizmodo 117605 visits/day (124)

5) HughHewitt.com 73303 visits/day (36)

6) www.AndrewSullivan.com - Daily Dish 62619 visits/day (8)

7) The Washington Monthly 55846 visits/day (11)

8) Defamer 50028 visits/day (678)

9) Wonkette 46772 visits/day (42)

10) Power Line 46493 visits/day (7)

11) The Smirking Chimp 41657 visits/day (273)

12) Allah Is In The House 39123 visits/day (15)

13) Blog for America 33746 visits/day (239)

14) Captain's Quarters Backup Site 29899 visits/day (3158)

15) Captain's Quarters 29899 visits/day (25)

16) Election Projection - 2004 Edition 26758 visits/day (174)

17) Taegan Goddard's Political Wire 25445 visits/day (94)

18) PoliPundit.com 23407 visits/day (240)

19) Belmont Club 23240 visits/day (39)

20) Drudge Retort: Red Meat for Yellow Dogs 20951 visits/day (2424)

21) Blogcritics 17919 visits/day (101)

22) Wizbang 17321 visits/day (14)

23) Wizbang: The First Daughters Interviewed In Vogue 17321 visits/day (34)

24) MyDD :: Due Diligence of Politics, Election Forecast & the World Today 15346 visits/day (208)

25) The Volokh Conspiracy - 14093 visits/day (9)

26) This Modern World 13978 visits/day (45)

27) Daly Thoughts & Dales' Electoral College Breakdown 2004 13781 visits/day (2566)

28) Daly Thoughts and Dales' Electoral College Breakdown 2004 13781 visits/day (1128)

29) Ace of Spades HQ 13664 visits/day (1634)

30) Ace of Spades HQ 13664 visits/day (96)

31) protein wisdom 13608 visits/day (1526)

32) protein wisdom 13608 visits/day (64)

33) TalkLeft: The Politics of Crime 12731 visits/day (43)

34) The Command Post - A Newsblog Collective 12463 visits/day (30)

35) The Command Post - Op-Ed 12463 visits/day (2005)

36) The Command Post 12463 visits/day (7073)

37) The Command Post - 2004 Presidential Election 12463 visits/day (433)

38) The Command Post - Global War On Terror 12463 visits/day (927)

39) pandagon.net - we only look young . . . 12180 visits/day (53)

40) onegoodmove: I thought these things might be clues 11065 visits/day (1384)

41) BeldarBlog 10707 visits/day (137)

42) BeldarBlog 10707 visits/day (325)

43) filchyboy 10391 visits/day (5104)

44) Vodkapundit - All the News That's Fit to Drink 10191 visits/day (26)

45) Brad DeLong's Semi-Daily Journal: A Weblog 10173 visits/day (46)

46) ScrappleFace 10147 visits/day (37)

47) IMAO 10005 visits/day (16)

48) Corante > The Importance of . . . 9848 visits/day (596)

49) Rising Hegemon 8868 visits/day (781)

50) Orcinus 8779 visits/day (78)

The ecosystem rating—the number in parentheses following the daily visitor traffic—is a different measure of blog reach, counting the number of inbound links to a blog from other sources.

But it is the traffic that matters, the number of visitors that really defines a blog's effectiveness as an agent of persuasion or dissemination. (Some blogs have two or more entries reflecting two or more entry points or different blogs. And please understand that a repeat "visitor" counts twice. Thus a compulsive visitor to ScrappleFace can account for tens or hundreds of its "visitors.")

The power of the blogs can only be understood through a comparison with old media. According to the Newspaper Association of America, in 2003 there were 217 daily newspapers with circulation over 50,000, of which 36 had circulation over 250,000 subscribers/readers. Less than 10 percent of all newspapers in the country account for more than half of the readership.

By contrast, the blogosphere list I've just shown has only 8 blogs with daily circulation above 50,000, and only 2 with circulation above 250,000.

But the blogosphere is less than five years old, and its growth rate is huge.

And some sites don't use the technology that allows this or other counting mechanisms to keep accurate score. Certainly **Lileks** receives more than fifty thousand visits per day, for example, but is not listed, and **National Review**'s **The Corner**'s readership must be above 250,000 per day.

If you compare even the mighty **Instapundit**—the uber-blog—with *USA Today*, the newspaper has a decided advantage. But think about the facts behind the paper's daily circulation of 2,136,000, or the *Wall Street Journal*'s circulation of 1,800,000 or the *New York Times*' circulation of 1,113,000. Every visitor to Professor Glenn Reynolds's site (the **Instapundit** is a distinguished professor of law at the University of Tennessee) reads at least a little of Glenn's work. Every single visitor is thus influenced by Glenn.

Contrast that impact between visitor and content with what happens when an average reader picks up any newspaper. He absorbs bits and pieces, with even the most-read features reaching only partial percentages of the entire circulation universe.

And the circulation trends for newspapers are terrible. In fact, the trends for all old media are terrible. A massive project for The Project for Excellence in Journalism, titled "The State of the News Media 2004," had more than two hundred pages of detailed findings that would make any old media shareholder weep. Doom is on the medium horizon, and in the short term there is only red ink. Some examples from the study's litany of woes afflicting old media and the good news for new media:

[FROM THE STUDY'S "NEWSPAPERS" SECTION]

Newspaper circulation is in decline.

The root problems go back to the late 1940s, when the percentage of Americans reading newspapers began to drop. But for years the U.S. population was growing so much that circulation kept rising and then, after 1970, remained stable.

That changed in 1990 when circulation began to decline in absolute numbers.

And the problem now appears to be more than fewer

people developing the newspaper habit. People who used to read every day now read less often. Some people who used to read a newspaper have stopped altogether.

Today, just more than half of Americans (54 percent) read a newspaper during the week, somewhat more (62 percent) on Sundays, and the number is continuing to drop.

Overall, some 55 million newspapers are sold each day, 59 million on Sunday.

At the same time, the number of newspapers in the country has been on a steady decline for even longer, dropping nearly 1 percent a year for now two decades to 1,457 in 2002.

[AND]

An exception to the 20-year slide in circulation has been national papers. *USA Today* has gone from a dead start to a circulation of 2.1 million daily. There is no exact measure of its impact on other dailies, but it clearly supplants local papers for convention goers and other travelers and represents competition to the other two nationally circulated dailies, the *New York Times* and the *Wall Street Journal*. Only 14 percent of *USA Today*'s circulation comes from home delivery. The *Wall Street Journal* holds its own, going back over the 2 million mark (with the addition in the most recent ABC audit of 300,000 paid subscribers to its online edition). Three-quarters of its circulation is attributed to home delivery and subscription sales spread across the country. Less obviously, the *New York Times* has gradually shifted from a metropolitan New York paper with some national circulation to having nearly half its circulation outside the New York City area.

In addition to a variety of free internet news sites and the rise of CNN and NPR, the competitive climate for providing a basic national and international news report has grown far tougher for the typical metropolitan or small-city newspaper. Together, the top 7 percent of the nation's newspapers (105 out of 1,457) command 55 percent of the total circulation.

[FROM THE STUDY'S "BIG THREE NEWSMAGAZINES" SECTION]

The readership data on the newsmagazines are not extensive. But combining what we know about the age, sex and income of the readers, one can draw very rough sketches of the audiences here. Among the big three newsmagazines, readership tends to be male. *Time* and *Newsweek* each have about two million more male readers than female, and *U.S. News* has three million more men than women thumbing through its pages.

Time, the oldest magazine of the three, has the youngest readership, an average age of 43.1. *Newsweek* is a bit older with an average age of 44.4. And *U.S. News* is the highest, with an average reader age of 45.

Newsweek's readers are slightly more affluent than Time's—average annual incomes of $66,739 and $65,697, respectively. *U.S. News* readers, while still above the industry average as a whole, have a slightly lower average income at $63,603. This finding is surprising because it is generally true that older readers have higher incomes. *U.S. News* seems to be an exception in this regard. Up until 2001, *U.S. News* actually had a higher average reader income, but in the past few years its figures have been surpassed by both *Time* and *Newsweek*.

[AND]

Time's circulation has fallen by 13 percent from 1988 to 2002. *U.S. News* has lost as well, also 13 percent from 1988 to 2003.

Newsweek has been the most stable of the three, experiencing a smaller drop of 3 percent in circulation since 1988. This disparity has significantly closed the gap between *Newsweek*, the historic No. 2, and *Time*, the long-time genre leader. The gap, 1.4 million in 1988, narrowed to 928,000 in 2001 and may have narrowed even more in 2002. Yet financially, this has not helped *Newsweek*—or hurt *Time*—as much as it once might have.

[FROM THE STUDY'S "NETWORK TELEVISION" SECTION]

A detailed look at the content of network news reveals that the evening newscasts are still network television's front page, and by traditional standards still home to its most serious journalism. Nearly 30 million people still watch the nightly news, and the programs remain profitable.

But the trend line is ominous. Evening news ratings have dropped 59 percent since their peak three decades ago. And the audience is aging—nearly 60 years old on average, while the average age of Americans is 35. The economics of evening newscasts is headed in a troubling direction.

[FROM THE STUDY'S "CABLE TELEVISION" SECTION]

Many ideas about cable's audience may also defy conventional wisdom. Contrary to press reports, the cable audience appears to have flattened since 2002. It is not growing. The medium kept none of the viewers it gained during the 2003 war in Iraq, and now that Fox and MSNBC are carried on most systems, continued growth may be harder to come by. As of early 2004, roughly 2.2 million viewers typically watched the three cable news networks every day in prime time, about the same number as in early 2002.

Fox, while the leader in ratings, also may not dominate as much as people imagine. Of the three channels, Fox is still gaining in ratings, while CNN and MSNBC are losing. At any given moment, Fox's audience is 60 percent higher than CNN's. Still, polling data continue to suggest that more people cite CNN as a news source overall. The problem in the numbers for CNN is that people are not all watching at the same time.

[AND]

In 2003, the median monthly viewership of Fox News was 770,000 daytime viewers and 1.4 million in prime time, 52 and 62 percent more, respectively, than CNN. In December 2003, Fox News averaged 1.4 million viewers in prime time, and 961,000 in daytime, both roughly 60 percent more than CNN. In conventional ratings terms, Fox News is well ahead.

[FROM THE STUDY'S "TALK RADIO" SECTION]

This would seem to fall in line with a January 2003 Gallup Poll that found that 22 percent of Americans relied on Talk Radio as their primary news source, double from four years ago.

While the percentage was viewed by some media organizations, and even some hosts of talk radio shows, as troubling, it is not surprising when the broader outline of radio as an information medium is considered. Radio is a medium that has evolved into one with an eye toward very specific formats. Because of its segmentation, despite the fact that formats are not always clearly and consistently delineated, it fosters a situation where listeners will go to the outlet of their own choosing. Many talk radio stations present themselves with a clear and well-defined position and philosophy that their programming holds closely to. It allows listeners, who might be inter-

84

ested only in a particular mindset or the opinions of a particular host, to select the portion of the dial that they feel best suits their needs or may, in fact, be filling a void they feel is left open in other media sources.

[FROM THE STUDY'S "THE INTERNET" SECTION]

In September 2003, over half of the people in the United States—150 million—went online, a record for Web use.

And half to two-thirds of those who go online use it at least some of the time to get news.

[AND]

Beyond the latest numbers, there is the question of whether online news use is still growing or whether it has peaked. Here, the data are conflicting.

Pew and Jupiter show the percentage of people that go online for news mostly growing. The UCLA study shows it fluctuating.

But even if the number is stable, if the number of people who go online overall is growing, then a steady percentage of news consumers would signify growth. Pinning this down, however, is difficult.

Pew Research Center data show online usage generally leveled off at around 62 percent in early 2001. The UCLA findings also show it basically flat since 2001. But Jupiter Research predicts that usage of the internet overall will grow because it expects household penetration—the percentage of homes connected to the internet—to rise from 63 percent in 2003 to 73 percent in 2007. That would be a gain of 14 million new online households, of which presumably more than half would become news consumers online.

[AND, FINALLY]

If Web usage does continue to grow, including going online to get the news, it raises a fundamental question: Will the Web kill old media? One longstanding worry among traditional news producers, particularly newspapers, is the fear that as more people turn to online news, it will sharply accelerate the pace at which their audience in the old media will shrink. Research in this area, though, suggests that the threat of technology may not be so cut and dry.

In 2002, nearly three-quarters of users (72 percent) said that they spent the same amount of time reading print newspapers today as they did before they began reading news online, according to Jupiter Research. Less than a quarter (22 percent) reported spending less time than before and a few, 3 percent, even said they spent more.

A similar pattern holds true for print magazines.

The Web may be having a greater negative impact on television news, but it still may not be as much as some people think. In the Jupiter study, 36 percent of internet users indicated that their television viewing time has decreased since going online, 14 percentage points more than for newspaper. About 61 percent said it was the same and 2 percent said it increased.

A 2000 survey from the Pew Research Center for the People and the Press also found that those who regularly went online reported watching less network television news than two years earlier. Fewer watched television news overall, and those who did watched less of it. Meanwhile, viewing among those who did not go online was unchanged.

Serious analysts of media trends will want to labor through all two-hundred-plus pages, and they can do so at **stateofthe newsmedia.org**. But what these brief excerpts are intended to underscore is this:

- Newspapers, the big three weekly newsmagazines, CNN and the networks: falling
- The blogosphere, the Fox News Channel, and talk radio: rising

That is the summary of the here and now. Let me explain why it happened.

THE MELTDOWN OF MAINSTREAM
MEDIA (MSM) AND WHERE ITS
AUDIENCE WENT

What has happened to journalism has happened to jihadism and is happening to investing and science and every other field. It happened first to journalism, and especially to political journalism, so if you can figure out what happened there, you can see what is happening elsewhere and what will happen to your world.

Most of America knows that elite journalism is staffed by people who are overwhelmingly way-left-of-center in their politics. If you don't believe that America believes that, or you want to argue over what "way-left-of-center" means, you have purchased the wrong book. You are still living in the land of the lost and don't want to move, so go buy Al Franken's or Michael Moore's latest and miss the revolution.

Because "news" is ultimately just a series of choices of a news organization over what to elevate beyond an individual's attention, the staffing matters a lot. Consider the news cycle. It hasn't changed from Homer's time.

Events or ideas happen. Events are concrete occurrences. Ideas are not.

An event or an idea interests an individual, who wishes other people to know of the event or the idea. So that individual tells others, either in person or via some other means of communication.

As the means of communication changed into engines of transmission that could turn a profit, the individual found it necessary to persuade others to help him or her spread the word of the event or the idea. Organizations developed to transmit news of events or ideas, and frequently they transmitted only the ideas they favored or news of events they liked. Bias had arrived.

In the twentieth century, mighty news organizations arose that began to police the process by which news of events or ideas spread. They hired reporters and editors and went "professional." Very few journalists worked alone. Hierarchies developed, and in their wake, career paths and editorial policies.

Because senior personnel tend to hire younger versions of themselves, over time self-selection produced generalized uniformity in outlook and worldview. Some credentials dominated, and just as résumés in the elite institutions tended to have the same set of institutions named, the bearers of those résumés tended to have the same political views. Hire fifty reporters from the Ivy League into the *New York Times*, *Time*, or the *Washington Post*, and 90 percent of those young reporters will arrive carrying roughly the same point of view on, say, the desirability of unlimited abortion rights even through the last trimester.

So the farm system was sending forth an army of recruits of like-minded would-be journalists off to the newspapers and radio stations and television networks and publishing houses. Where they found the pay wasn't very good. And the work was often not much fun and very often overlooked. High-achieving individuals can be motivated by nonmonetary "status perks," or by idealism, but the former had better be consistent and powerful and the latter is likely to burn low as mortgage payments and children arrive. Many of these under-twenty-five-year-old go-getters slowly embraced disappointment, learned envy of their counterparts in the law and business, and their natural hostility to conservative politics morphed into resentment of the party the people of means and achievement in the marketplace generally belonged to: the GOP.

And hostility grew and became entrenched and then generational. And Nixon gave the agenda journalists a reason to hate the GOP more. And Reagan gave the next generation of agenda journalists a reason to double down on condescension. And soon elite media had drifted off into the land of the far left.

Again, honest members of elite media will tell you this is true. They will also tell you that they work hard to overcome their own biases and their own preferences, and that they and their colleagues do. But they will admit to close friends—as many have admitted to me—that 90 percent of their colleagues in the newsrooms of the *New York Times*, the *Boston Globe*, the *Los Angeles Times*, the *Washington Post, Time,* and *Newsweek*, CBS, NBC, ABC, and CNN and their affiliated cable channels, plus most elite magazines such as *Harper's, Atlantic,* the *New Republic,* and the New York publishing houses voted for Gore or Nader in 2000 and Kerry in 2004.

But they don't and they can't admit the above to the public, even though the consumer of news and information knows that. Since the consumers of news and information are hungry for reliable, unfiltered information on which to base decisions, they are open to new, trustworthy sources of that information.

They also demand speed. Who bases an investment decision on last week's *Wall Street Journal*? Who doesn't, before buying a stock, check some internet service for the price and late-breaking headlines?

In other words, "reliable information" has come to mean "very recent reliable information."

That's where the blogosphere comes in.

Most of the people who read **Hugh Hewitt** do so because they trust me and they don't have the time or inclination to scour the political, national, and international news every day or hour or edit what they read. I am a shortcut, a convenience. So is **Instapundit**. So are **PowerLine, Captain's Quarters, Polipundit, Lileks, The Corner, The Daily Standard** (at **WeeklyStandard.com**), **Galley Slaves, Best of the Web**, etc., etc., etc. So are the blogs of the left for the people of the left.

And between the best of us, we are constantly updating and refining the news upon which people base their news judgments: which elected official to vote for, which to send money to or praise to their friends, or which bills to support or political organizations to join. The bloggers are performing a cueing function, prompting people's actions in hundreds of thousands of ways. Talk radio does the very same thing when it is well produced, but talk radio can only be current during the hours the program is live. Thus *The Hugh Hewitt Show* is very reliable between the hours of 6 and 9 PM, Monday through Friday in the East, 3 to 6 PM in the West. My program is tape-delayed in places such as Philadelphia, Chicago, and Dallas, so it is somewhat less reliable than it is in Boston, Cleveland, the Twin Cities, Denver, or Seattle, Portland, San Francisco, Sacramento, Los Angeles, San Diego, or Honolulu, where it is live. Stuff happens at 9 PM at night in New York that surges to the top of the headlines. When my show is tape-delayed, it cannot compete with breaking news.

The victims of this demand for reliable information are the

purveyors of information believed to be stale—the newspapers, the networks, the newsweeklies—for the same reason a tape-delayed radio show is less trustworthy than a live broadcast. They can't keep up. They lose the race every day because their production timeline requires them to file stories before I am off the air, the stories I can report while on the air. I try to pound this home by making sure that I report on every story likely to be a headline in tomorrow's newspapers and then confirm to my audience that the newspapers have once again given them yesterday's news today. I want the audience to know that again and again they are getting stale news in the morning paper.

Add to the reality that they are selling the news equivalent of day-old bread—or with *Time* and *Newsweek,* week-old rolls—the corrosive factor of crippled credibility due to perceived bias. Every time bias can be shown to exist within a major news organization, all of MSM suffers as the public absorbs another lesson in the unreliability of the bigs. The effect is diffuse, even though the perps are specific.

When Rathergate broke in September 2004, many callers to my show demanded that I bring up CBS's earlier sin of contriving to explode GM cars to make a point about gas tank dangers. When I pointed out that the crash fraud had been perpetrated by NBC's *Dateline* program, it hardly mattered a bit. "All networks alike" is the common understanding, and with good reason. They are all alike, like three towering mansions from a long-ago era, all of which are somewhat tumbled down, in need of repair, certainly not places you'd want to move into without major renovations. Each scar on big media is a scar on all big media. They are all slow, and they are all scarred.

Some of the defenders of the bigs will grumble about the unfairness of what is happening, especially the assumptions of my brief explanation of the Decline and Fall of the Mainstream Media Empire. Grumble all they want, the vandals are still over the walls. It is over. They *are* slow. They *are* perceived as way-left. And they have been caught cheating in the production of their product.

There are now alternatives, and they developed in the blink of a media eye, beginning with the launch of Rush Limbaugh's radio program in the late 1980s after the collapse of the Fairness Doctrine. That artificial doctrine, mandating evenhandedness in broadcasting of news and political opinion, had served as a deep freeze for debate for decades, forcing cautious radio execs to serve their politics in vanilla pudding. "Public affairs" broadcasting was the dreary backwater of the broadcast world, until the Fairness Doctrine was repealed. Then Rush strode out and began to speak his mind, and tens of millions of Americans said, "Hey, that's what I think!" And his show exploded. And imitators, including me, followed. AM radio became the staging ground for an assault on MSM, a proof text for the business types who wanted models showing profitability. And then FOX News arrived, and from then forward there was on the small screen a place to find a few conservative voices mixed in with the liberal voices, and a few anchors like Hume and later Cavuto and Gibson and Smith, who were perceived by a large portion of the audience as fair. *And balanced.*

At first MSM and its allies in academia fought back by blasting Rush and second-generation talkers as militia-right-wing, famously in the case of Bill Clinton's assault on Limbaugh after the Oklahoma City massacre.

This did not work, as listeners understood Limbaugh was not far-right, and that the charge was a smear. The polarization of news consumption continued, and the increasing vehemence of the charges and countercharges of bias and "the politics of hate" simply accelerated the sorting process of media outlets into "trustworthy" and "biased" categories. The left, resentful that a market of idea outlets had arrived, grew shrill. First Limbaugh, then FOX News, then my colleagues and I on the broadcast dial simply grew. The *Weekly Standard* was launched. Conservative publishing houses like Regnery and Thomas Nelson prospered.

And then the blogs arrived like cavalry coming over the hill. The attempt by MSM to fight back against the emerging center-right media was doomed. Go back and read the article about swarming in chapter 1. MSM can no longer control the battle-field, dictating who gets to participate, when stories are released, and who has the final say.

The public has the final say. There is no going back, only an endless effort to capture and keep audience based on credibility.

Now the dynamics of the new news environment are spread-ing over into all fields in which information matters. Gatekeepers in all fields, even those not yet under assault, will be shortly. I haven't a clue how the music industry functions, but I know that the practices of the past are doomed.

I don't know how life-insurance salesmen used to practice their trade, but that's over now.

Criminal enterprises may have at one time been aggressive in their exploitation of gaps in the public safety infrastructure, but the best of the criminal minds are figuring out the Net's applicability, as my ten thousand e-mails from ex–secretaries of state in remote Nigerian provinces and offers to buy overseas prescription meds attest. Who knows what the real talented bad guys are up to?

Every single information hierarchy is under siege, whether you know it or not. The Cimbri gave Rome a warning because as a mass of barbarians they moved slowly south, thus allowing Rome the opportunity to recover from one military disaster after another and finally put Gaius Marius in the field with tactics developed to destroy the horde.

But most folks don't see their enemies coming. The enemy could be the blogosphere, and the early warning system of the enemy's approach could also be the blogosphere.

The power of networked information isn't confined to folks intent on doing good or sworn to nonviolent means of political change or to legal means of making money. The best example of networked "evildoers" is of course Al Qaeda and its spin-off.

In an article for the July 26, 2004, *New Yorker*, Lawrence Wright carefully reconstructed the burst and spread of jihadist ideology, and deep into the article he focused on the use of the internet in propelling fanaticism into its growth age: "The internet provides confused young Muslims in Europe with a virtual community. Those who cannot adapt to their new homes discover on the internet a responsive and compassionate forum."

"The internet stands in for the idea of the ummah, the mythologized Muslim community," Marc Sageman, the psychiatrist and former CIA officer, said. "The internet makes this ideal community concrete, because one can interact with it." He compares this virtual ummah to romantic conceptions of nationhood, which inspire people not only to love their country but to die for it.

"The internet is the key issue," Gilles Kepel, a prominent Arabist and a professor at the Institut d'Études Politiques in Paris, told me recently. "It erases the frontiers between the dar al-Islam and the dar al-Kufr. It allows the propagation of a universal norm, with an internet Sharia and fatwa system." Kepel was speaking of the Islamic legal code, which is administered by the clergy. Now one doesn't have to be in Saudi Arabia or Egypt to live under the rule of Islamic law. "Anyone can seek a ruling from his favorite sheikh in Mecca," Kepel said. "In the old days, one sought a fatwa from the sheikh who had the best knowledge. Now it is sought from the one with the best website."

To a large extent, Kepel argues, the internet has replaced the Arabic satellite channels as a conduit of information and communication. "One can say that this war against the West started on television," he said, "but, for instance, with the decapitation of the poor hostages in Iraq and Saudi Arabia, those images were propagated via webcams and the internet. A jihadi subculture has been created that didn't exist before 9/11."

Because the internet is anonymous, Islamist dissidents are less susceptible to government pressure. "There is no signature," Kepel said. "To some of us who have been trained as classicists, the cyber-world appears very much like the time before Gutenberg. Copyists used to add their own notes into a text, so you never know who was the real author."

How fast has the growth of this jihadist cyber-culture been? Wright continued:

"Gabriel Weimann, a senior fellow at the United States Institute of Peace, has been monitoring terrorist websites for seven years. 'When we started, there were only twelve sites,' he told me. 'Now there are more than four thousand.'" Every known terrorist group maintains more than one website, and often the sites are in different languages. "You can download music, videos, donate money, receive training," Weimann said. "It's a virtual training camp." There are two online magazines associated with Al Qaeda, Sawt al-Jihad (Voice of Jihad) and Muaskar al-Battar (Camp al-Battar), which feature how-to articles on kidnapping, poisoning, and murdering hostages. Specific targets, such as the Centers for Disease Control in Atlanta, or FedWire, the money-clearing system operated by the Federal Reserve Board, are openly discussed. "We do see a rising focus on the U.S.," Weimann told me. "But some of this talk may be fake—a scare campaign."

While this is obviously the most troubling manifestation of the blogosphere's power—and these jihadist sites are very much a part of the blogosphere, though condemned by most American and Western bloggers—it would be delusional to think that this is an isolated case study. Anyone with any agenda can use blogs to advance that agenda—and probably are already trying to do so. That most bloggers eschew violence is no guarantee that those who embrace violence will not be as skilled or even more skilled than law-abiding bloggers in gaining audiences and directing audiences via their blogs.

Jihadists have reached for cyber-sources because the means by which the news traveled in MSM lost credibility for them. They came to see media as dominated by Western ownership or dictatorial rulers of authoritarian states. So they invented their own.

Any group with a grievance against MSM now has the ability to at least attempt a breakout for its views. One of the true disasters of MSM conformity over the years is the short shrift it has collectively given to the legitimately aggrieved around the world. When CNN's Eason Jordan admitted in an April 2003 *New York Times* column that his network had suppressed news of Saddam's brutality, some in media criticism circles tried to find a way to excuse it. The Poynter Institute's Bob Steele, in an April 17, 2003, commentary at **Poynter Online** wrote:

Here's a journalism ethics case that will go in the books. It's an example of moral complexity with multiple dilemmas that defy simple answers. CNN chief news executive Eason Jordan is at the center of a controversy triggered by his revelation that CNN did not report some stories about atrocities in Iraq over the past dozen years. Jordan says reporting them would have risked getting innocent people killed.

A victim of Saddam during the period of Saddam's brutality and CNN's complicity might look at all MSM and conclude it could not be trusted—ever. That victim, or his or her family or friends, might not think of CNN's complicity in Saddam's evil as an "example of moral complexity with multiple dilemmas." They would conclude that it was toadyism. And they would be right. They would view CNN, and all the networks staffed by American elites, as Americans by and large view Al Jazeera.

That's the jihadists' conclusion, and their network of websites and bulletin boards is their response. Did that network give rise to the legions of free-agent terrorists, or did the ideology transform the medium of the blogosphere to its ends? It doesn't matter, because the network is now there. We can only wonder if a fair and balanced MSM had been attentive to the reality of Saddam from 1979 forward, or before him Khomeni, or before him the communists of Southeast Asia or the machinations of Stalin or the early years of Hitler, how many lives would have been saved and conflicts and humanitarian disasters avoided. Media's power is in alerting free peoples to dangers, and in each case mentioned, the MSM did nothing of the sort.

Reporting on world affairs and international conflicts is just one part of the vast information flow. In field after field, dominant information possessors and distributors have fallen victim to the temptation to package the information they dispense in ways that benefit themselves as opposed to their customers. This is "self-dealing," and once revealed, it is an instant marker of dishonesty. The blogosphere now exists as the most convenient means of exposing such self-dealing.

Visit **FundPolice.com** at some point. Full disclosure: the founder of **Fund Police** is a client of mine on the radio, and he pays me a small sum to voice his ads. **Fund Police** is a site that lists story after story on mutual-fund practices that have caught the attention of prosecutors and securities regulators. The long-hidden practices of that industry, which led to abuse of investors' interests generally in order to benefit fund operators and preferred clients, have been ousted, and with exposure came a new hostility to mutual funds on the part of consumers. Sites such as **Fund Police** try to gain consumer attention and collect the allegiance of investors who feel betrayed by the practices of the big funds they unthinkingly trusted for many years.

What **Fund Police** has done for the mutual funds, **ScienceBlog.com** is attempting to do for science news and communities. **Science Blog** may not succeed—there is plenty of competition from **NewScientist.com** and so on—but one or more blogs or independent sites will succeed in gathering the traffic of thousands of PhDs and researchers of one sort or another because it will become a convenient shortcut to the news these cultures use. Jihadists, investors, scientists—all alike. They all want information they can trust, and trust must be earned and is easily lost.

Existing hierarchies can choose to ignore the massive changes under way, as MSM and Western political elites chose to ignore the polibloggers and the jihadists respectively. When the shock comes, then, they will be wholly unprepared and may not be able to recover.

Or they can begin to plan for the changes. Let me give you one example of adaptation, this from the world of the faithbloggers.

Faithbloggers are the men and women of the Judeo-Christian world who write primarily about their faith, or from a perspective that almost always draws upon their faith. Certainly other faiths have bloggers, but I am most familiar with these bloggers, and the term *faithblogger* was first used in connection with them.

Over at **blogs4God.com**—formerly Martin Roth's "Semi-Definitive List of Christian Blogs"—there are eight categories of Christian blogs: apologia, church polity, journals, metablogs, ministries, pundits, techblogs, and "zines." At this writing, Mr. Roth had collected and categorized 1,291 sites. Find the weblog alliance **Blogdom of God** and you will find an even more complex charting of the cybergeography of faithbloggers. There is also the **ChristianTop1000.com**, which is a simple traffic count for sites categorizing themselves as "Christian," many of which are weblogs, others of which are conventional sites lacking the "frequent posting by one or more unique voices."

As you can see, the blogosphere has been noticed by forward-thinking people of faith.

One of these faithbloggers is Mark D. Roberts, whose blog is found at **MarkDRoberts.com**. He began it on December 21, 2003, and he has of this writing attracted over 120,000 visitors in less than ten months. Roberts's success could have been predicted. He's the author of three highly respected and successful books. He's a "double Harvard," having taken his undergraduate and PhDs from Cambridge. And he's a prolific scribbler and seminary teacher, as well as a speaker in wide demand in Presbyterian and other reformed circles. He preaches each week to a few hundred at his congregation, so he is constantly thinking about communicating. A blog was a natural evolution of his ministry.

But not just because he is prolific. I also believe he saw that a giant struggle would get under way in the blogosphere among differing Christian views of correct theology, as well as between theists and atheists, and Trinitarian Christians and other world religions. And he sensed, correctly, that many would be called to the blogosphere but that few would be trained in theology.

Here is an excerpt from one of his sermons on truth:

> It's important to mention the centrality of authoritative teaching in the church because this also goes against the grain of our culture. We tend more and more to reject so-called authorities and to prefer our own insights to those of the experts. You'll find many "cutting edge" churches these days that minimize the role of authoritative teaching, favoring instead a more collegial effort to seek the truth. Now I'm a big fan of inductive Bible study and group discussion. It's both wonderful and even essential to a healthy church. But there still is a need for people with the proper training, experience, and gifting to teach with recognized authority.
>
> I first ran into the rejection of this kind of authority when I was beginning my college ministry at the First Presbyterian Church of Hollywood. I was leading a Bible study about Jesus, focusing on his proclamation of the kingdom of God. I was teaching the collegians what Jesus meant when he referred to the kingdom, pointing out the meaning of Jesus' Aramaic words, the prophetic context in the Old Testament, and the expectations for the kingdom among Jews in the time of Jesus.
>
> In the midst of the study a young woman interrupted me. Claire, I'll call her, said, "I hear what you're saying about the

kingdom of God, but I feel this isn't right. What Jesus was really talking about was having a sense of God's presence. That's why he said that 'the kingdom of God is within you.'" I acknowledged Claire's point and tried to affirm what I could, but I also showed her what Jesus really meant when he said "the kingdom of God is within you," pointing again to the meaning of the original language, etc.

Claire wasn't convinced, however. "But that's not what I feel is right. The kingdom of God is really about feeling God's presence." When I tried once again to stretch her understanding, she became upset. "You're telling me my feelings aren't correct, and you have no right to tell me I can't feel as I do." At this point Claire began to cry and rushed out of the room. The other collegians were angry with me. "How can you say Claire is wrong?" they objected. "Her feelings are just as valid as yours!" I thought to myself: Perhaps if I had run out of the room crying they would have sided with me against Claire!

In telling this story, I'm certainly not suggesting that I handled the matter perfectly. But my point is that biblical truth isn't simply up for grabs. What Jesus actually meant by the kingdom of God isn't so much a matter of how someone feels about it as it is about the facts of Jesus' ministry, understood in their historical and theological context. Claire, who certainly had a genuine and deep relationship with God, needed me to help her grow in that relationship, both in truth and in depth.

Claire probably has a blog. So do many other well-meaning Christians with lousy theology. So do many cultists, and so do many ardent atheists. My guess is that one of the reasons that Roberts added a blog to his already busy schedule was to establish one outpost in the blogosphere where theology of the reformed variety—backed by scholarship and pastoral experience—could be available to those searching for it.

In other words, Roberts saw change coming to the church and set out to help the church adapt to that change. So did Dr. Albert Mohler, who blogs at **Crosswalk.com** (**crosswalk.com/ news/weblogs/mohler**), Professor John Mark Reynolds of Biola University, who blogs at **JohnMarkReynolds.com**, and Joe Carter, who blogs at **Evangelical Outpost** (**EvangelicalOutpost.com**). There are many others. They get it.

USING THE NEW MEDIA

The old information monopoly had an enormous ability to decide where and when news would be "news." That gatekeeping function is gone, and blogs have rushed in to decide for themselves what matters. The episodes detailed earlier were the first few rounds of conflict between MSM and bloggers. What is coming soon—perhaps even in the summer of 2005—are clashes between competing blog camps. The perfect interblog storm is brewing and will break when the next Supreme Court nominee is sent from the White House to the presidency.

In fact, all future Supreme Court nominations are going to ignite blog wars as poliblogs of the left and right scramble to analyze, categorize, canonize, or demonize at least the next few nominees. Newspapers and electronic media have never been that good at covering Supreme Court nominees or the battles that have marked them, unless the controversy became highly focused, as it did with Clarence Thomas and Anita Hill's allegations.

Because there are so many accomplished lawyers and law professors who are blogging, they will quickly establish story lines and mine and excerpt the nominee's opinions, articles, and internet-available after-dinner speeches. Every electronic mark ever put down by the nominee will be unearthed and instantly processed and debated with abandon. Because the stakes are so high with such a closely divided court, the energy that will be expended on trying to shape public opinion will be enormous. Left and right polibloggers will follow the lawbloggers closely, capturing the information they can use to advance their agendas. The blogs will move much more quickly, and with much greater authority than MSM. They will make or break the nominee.

Which is why perhaps future presidents ought to put three or four names out for collective blog vetting before a final choice is made. The White House Counsel's Office and the Department of Justice are staffed by fine lawyers with great capacity for research and analysis.

But their number and their energy are finite. Harnessing the power of the blogosphere to provide early assessments of nominees' strengths and nominees' weaknesses would be a bold embrace of open-source journalism, turning its potentially destructive power into an asset to be used in determining the best decision on the appropriate nominee.

Similarly, any potential controversy may best be managed by posing it as a hypothetical first to the blogs if the controversy's arc cannot be judged because of imperfect information. Would Coca-Cola have been well served, had the blogosphere existed on April 23, 1985, to pose the question of New Coke to the relentlessly opinionated world of first-person open journalism? A thousand such opportunities exist to harness the new media, if the platforms are built from which such tests can be launched.

WHY DO BLOGGERS BLOG?
AND WHY IT MATTERS TO YOU

Why did cavemen paint on walls? I don't care. They have nothing to do with me.

But I do care why bloggers blog.

Two reasons: to persuade, and to leave a record of having been there. Both are vain efforts in the long haul. Both efforts have never not been hallmarks of humanity. "All is vanity and a chasing after wind," says Ecclesiastes (1:14).

But in real time, both efforts are a blast.

What is new about the blogosphere is that there are no barriers to entry to a world offering a nearly limitless audience. Key point: *offering,* not guaranteeing. Anyone can post, and if it is worth reading, it will be read. There is a vast audience of wisdom/entertainment seekers. Whether your product is economic analysis, NASCAR boosterism, sexual gossip, or political smack talk, the blogosphere will allow you a chance to peddle your text wares.

Many, many are the blogs that will go unread except for a

college roommate or a brother-in-law. Some people will grow tired and abandon the effort. Others will muscle on despite low traffic. What you have to be concerned about are those folks who arrive out of nowhere and surge to tens of thousands and then hundreds of thousands of daily visits.

That's the key number, btw. Page views are like Confederate currency: fun to have but worthless. Give me unique eyeballs over Poindexters with patience any day.

Some folks in the blogosphere don't keep count of their traffic. **Lileks,** for instance. *Minneapolis Star Tribune* columnist. *Newhouse News Service* columnist. Humorist. Father of Gnat. Blogger extraordinaire.

Lileks is read by everyone of consequence in the blogosphere. I mean everyone. Because he's funny. And wise. He's worth his weight in gold. Hire him away from the *Star Tribune (Strib)* if he hasn't been hired away already.

But he never kept count. I always have. I had the advantage of the radio show, so I could cajole listeners into becoming readers, but not James. He tallied blog traffic the old-fashioned way: he earned it with good humor and a love for his daughter that connected with everyone who loved kids for even a day.

And when **Lileks** turned into a warblogger, he made his bones. His audience swelled as **Lileks** turned tremendous writing skills to the issues of the war and a post-9/11 world. He was a humorist columnist, a lifestyle columnist, but suddenly he was a *warblogger,* an amorphous category that included anyone from any part of the political spectrum who advocated a robust prosecution of the Global War on Terror, which became acronymized on the blogosphere as GWOT.

He wasn't alone. On the left coast Roger L. Simon, a director, screenwriter, and mystery novelist who had begun his own blog to promote his Moses Wine detective novels, found himself, as a cutting-edge "9/11 Democrat," and also increasingly isolated in a Hollywood community exercising its traditional choice of being wrong loudly and out of step with America greatly.

Though he blogged on at considerable peril to his professional prospects, Simon was never less alone because of the vast audience he earned for himself, reaching into the tens of thousands a day. He was invited to blog the Republican National Convention and returned to his hometown to do so.

Why did Charles Johnson of **Little Green Footballs** start? It doesn't matter. What matters is the size of his audience and the rapidity with which his bulletins on various aspects of Islamofascism spread with breathtaking speed across the internet.

Why did **PowerLine** get under way? As a continuation of the authors' love of public policy and politics, a love that had led them to write for various publications and newspapers over the years. Their hobby became a subject of national importance when they added gasoline to the fire begun on **Free Republic** concerning Rathergate.

In the past, opinion and news purveyors always had to persuade someone to be allowed to attempt to persuade someone. When I wanted to write about the race for the United States Senate in 1992 in California, for example, I had to persuade the deputy editor of the editorial page to publish my take on the contest between Bruce Herschenson and Barbara Boxer. He made edits I didn't like, but I was in no position to argue. The *Times* had a near-monopoly on the means of communicating political writing to any decent-sized audience. And when Boxer operative Bob Mulholland slaundered Bruce in the last days of the campaign, I and other Herschenson supporters had no means of striking back via the publication of rebuttals to the lies and distortions told then.

A dozen years later and any such sneak attack—such as the CBS forged memos of September 2004—will be immediately exposed and in fact cripple the side who is allied with whoever launched the sneak attack.

Bloggers are the same people they were a few years ago. But now they don't have to persuade anyone to be allowed to persuade anyone. The information monopoly, especially in the world of politics, is shattered because the gatekeepers have lost their authority.

Polibloggers blog for exactly the same reason—*and with exactly the same authority*—as columnists such as Thomas Freidman, E. J. Dionne, Charles Krauthhammer, and George Will, to name but four of the biggest names, write columns. And for exactly the same reason as Bill Clinton offered for his affair with Monica Lewinsky: because he could.

Writers write for the same reasons today as they did in Homer's age. Blogging is just a new means of transmitting that writing, one that bypasses completely all editors.

The public becomes the editor.

And that's a very good thing unless you got paid or derived status from being an editor.

The credibility of blogs depends on their timeliness and accuracy, but invariably, the qualifications of the bloggers matter as well. Here are some thumbnail sketches of the most influential of the polibloggers as 2005 gets under way.

Who are they? **DailyKos (dailykos.com)** received two bachelor degrees from Northern Illinois University (with majors in philosophy, political science, and journalism) and a JD from Boston University School of Law (emphasis in trial litigation). He is a resident of San Francisco, working in the tech industry. He is also an Army veteran.

He is also an off-the-wall lefty, willing to say anything, including a memorable meltdown that declared that American contractors murdered in Fallujah in the spring of '04 were mercenaries. Kos gets 1.6 million—that's *million*—visitors a month.

Glenn Reynolds is the **Instapundit.** He is a law professor at the University of Tennessee. His chief interest is in the intersection between advanced technologies and individual liberty. With huge traffic, he drives many issues on the web.

Atrios is the blogging name of Duncan Black, a self-described "recovering economist" living in Center City Philadelphia: **http://atrios.blogspot.com/2003/09/brief-bio.html.** Hard left. Incoherent, actually. But big traffic.

Wonkette (**wonkette.com**) is a gossip site. Funny. Very ribald. But a gossip site. Nothing more. 80,000 visitors a day and growing. Gossip is a growth field. Owned by **Gawker,** a pioneer in blogging, a sort of publishing house of blogs, many of which fail the taste test, but most of which attract huge traffic.

And, finally: **PowerLine** (**PowerLineBlog.com**). Three lawyers as contributors, and hugely influential. John H. Hinderaker, Scott W. Johnson, and Paul Mirengoff are the writers. John and Scott are both attorneys in Minneapolis. Paul is an attorney with Atkin, Gump in Washington, D.C. All are contributors to the Claremont Institute, a serious think tank based in Claremont, California (**www.Claremont.org**). They are also the senior members of The Northern Alliance—a group of Minnesota-based blogs that includes **Lileks, Captain's Quarters, SCSU Scholars, Shot In The Dark,** and **Spitbull,** and which are collectively changing the way Minnesota thinks. Did I mention **Fraters Libertas** (**FratersLibertas.com**)? They are also part of The Northern Alliance, in the way that the crazy aunt in the basement is part of the family.

Keep in mind that while this handful of blogs has enormous numbers of visitors, there are many other neoblogs that far outstrip them. James Lileks's **The Bleat** is a one-post-a-day site, but it has huge traffic and incredible influence throughout the blogosphere. **National Review**'s **The Corner, KerrySpot,** and **David Frum's Diary** are all blogs of a sort, and National Review's overall site has an enormous number of visitors and extremely high trust value. The power of such a site is that it combines both traffic and trust.

Also keep in mind that newcomers with talent find their sites are quickly mentioned and adopted, with staggering rises in traffic as a result. Ed Morrissey's **Captain's Quarters** and the group blog **Polipundit** earned large followings during election 2004, as did **INDC Journal** (INDCJournal.com), **BeldarBlog, Ann Althouse** (althouse.blogspot.com), and Tom McGuire's **JustOne Minute** (justoneminute.typepad.com). The early bloggers such as **The Volokh Conspiracy** (Volokh.com) and Virginia Postrel maintained their followings, but the new entrants found a warm welcome from a rapidly expanding group of blog users. In a market where new customers appear daily—many coming from talk radio and other media that have alerted news consumers to the blogosphere's existence—new entrants can quickly establish and defend a brand.

Traffic is not the only thing to consider, a lesson I learned from David Sifry, founder of **Technorati.com**. Technorati is an extraordinary tool for tracking the rise of stories on the blogosphere as well as cross-referencing posts. If I want to see who is commenting on **Hugh Hewitt**'s latest post, for example, I type my URL into the Technorati search engine and presto, a list of blogs referencing my own appears. There are other similar search engines, but I use Technorati almost exclusively because David's got a big brain and thinks a lot about the nature of the rapidly changing medium.

At the Democratic National Convention where we met, David first tutored me on a crucial concept: "the power of the tail." It is a counterintuitive idea, so it takes a couple of moments to get, but once gotten, it cannot be abandoned without losing a glimpse of the extraordinary power of the medium.

"The tail" is simply the 95 to 99 percent of blogs that are not giant traffic getters. These are low- or medium-traffic generators, some getting ten visitors a day, some a hundred, some a few hundred. Their traffic is steady, but it isn't growing at a great rate, if at all.

David calls this vast number of blogs "the tail" because on a graph of where traffic is located, the first few score blogs show huge numbers, but quickly the line plummets but goes on and on, out through the universe of millions and millions of blogs—the very long tail of the blogosphere.

"The power of the tail" is the aggregate number of visitors, not to any particular blog within the tail, but collectively to all blogs on the tail, and the fact that these low- or medium-traffic blogs generally enjoy the trust of their visitors. Say the web traffic on any given day for the top ten blogs is two million visitors. Of course, given the enormous influence of these two million visitors, that's an audience a would-be opinion influencer must try to target.

But there is huge, huge audience out among the tail. If a point of view or product makes its way throughout most of the blogs in the tail, the audience for that point of view or product will far outstrip even the largest audience for the biggest blogs. Because visitors to these low-traffic blogs are attached to them for some reason—friends, families, coworkers—the impact of the commentary will be higher than if a stranger visits, say, **Infinite**

Monkeys (InfiniteMonkeysBlog.com) on a link lark. Further, repeat visitors are signaling trust via their investment of time. If the tail picks up a meme, the spread of that meme will be instantaneous and is likely to be believed by the audience unique to the low- or moderate-traffic blogs.

The low- or moderate-traffic blog fills a niche parallel to that of the PTA newsletter, the church bulletin, and perhaps the local free weekly that covers high-school sports. Once the technology develops to identify who is reading these blogs and where, watch for marketing gurus to figure out how to use blogs to penetrate a particular market such as San Diego or Des Moines. And look for attempts to try to corral the attention of the tail.

I began a feature of **Hugh Hewitt** called first "The Virtual Symposium," and then the "Vox Blogoli" in October 2004. I would put a question out and link all bloggers who answered it. This had the effect of focusing the attention of a few hundred blogs on questions that interested me because low-traffic blogs especially valued the link I offered and the traffic it might produce. The first symposium produced about forty different postings across the blogosphere, the next about double. The third—which asked "Why vote for George Bush and what's wrong with John Kerry?"—more than three hundred links. The question was designed to get a great number of smaller bloggers talking about the election and hopefully influencing their low to moderate level of readers.

Anyone with traffic can do the same thing. There is one key to the tail: Build a high-traffic blog and then offer links to other bloggers who cover what you would like covered. Other techniques will emerge, such as contests or awards, but the tail matters—and whoever figures out ways to drive messages into that tail will have achieved an enormous advantage for his point of view or product.

A final word on ideology and the blogosphere: there is currently a talent gap. The political left is seriously behind in the promotion and development of bloggers with insight and good humor. It may be that the early entrants such as **DailyKos, Atrios,** and Joshua Micah Marshall's **Talking Points Memo** have set a tone of self-importance combined with coarseness that has repelled would-be bloggers, or that Peter Principle bloggers with energy but not enough talent have taken up valuable shelf space. Either way, there is definitely a talent gap. And there is a great deal more encouragement among the center-right for new entrants, a sort of "Welcome aboard, now grab an oar" attitude that applauds the arrival of, say, **Galley Slaves** or **The Hedgehog Report (davidwissing.com)** as fellow workers, a generosity of spirit that I just don't see on the left side of the spectrum. This is a decided advantage for my center-right ideology, and I hope my fellow scribblers on the center-right side of the spectrum continue to, in the words of Alex Haley found on his tombstone, "Find the good and praise it."

Joe Carter of **Evangelical Outpost** started a website called **Hugh Hewitt Inspired Blogs (hewittinspired.blogspot.com)**. He did so when something I wrote encouraged him to get blogging. The list at that site now numbers more than one hundred, an achievement from my writing probably more lasting than anything else I have accomplished by scribbling. I think the best goal of a blogger is to get others into the craft, even if they are direct competitors. Every good blog will bring new readers to the blogosphere, just as anchor stores bring traffic to the mall. Everybody wins when the customer base expands. Believe it.

PART III

EARTHQUAKES, HURRICANES, AND TORNADOES—WHAT'S AN EXECUTIVE TO DO?

7

ESTABLISHING A DEFENSE

Certain natural phenomena are predictable in only the most general sense. There is a hurricane season every year, but as Florida discovered in 2004, some seasons are far worse than others. Earthquakes are a certainty in California, but even major shakers are soon forgotten and the unpleasant prospect of the Big One packed away in the back of the mind along with the preparedness kit. And tornadoes—who can do anything about tornadoes except dig a cellar and keep a radio on when the sky gets dark?

Despite the irregularities of these events, modern civilization has taken quite a few steps to better prepare an entire region against their catastrophic impact. Thus we have continually evolving building codes, earthquake drills, evacuation plans, flood and earthquake insurance, and yes, those cellars. Would any executive in any company in Los Angeles feel good about a management team that didn't have an earthquake response plan in place with mandated reviews? Do you think Disneyland has trained and retrained its employees about automatic responses to a major temblor? There's a reason we have a National Hurricane Center and that we chart the paths of storms as they advance toward the eastern seaboard or the Gulf Coast. And there's an emergency warning system in place, from sirens to scrolls on the bottom of televisions to beeps over the radio, that blankets the tornado zones in the Midwest.

These are the very expensive infrastructures of safety and injury prevention. Add to their number all firehouses and police cars, National Guard units and civil defense shelters, and now the vast apparatus of Homeland Security in an age of terror. That a threat has not yet and may never materialize is not an adequate response to an environment in which a threat's sudden appearance could be catastrophic.

A blog swarm around your business or organization could be catastrophic. Thus far only CBS has really felt the impact of a devastating opinion storm generated by a blog swarm, but the damage done to its brand was immense, and its viewership crashed in the aftermath of Ra^(th)ergate. CBS was unprepared for the blog swarm.

If your organization is unprepared for a blog swarm, take steps to prepare it, as unlikely as that swarm seems at this moment. You may not think that you are vulnerable, but given the rate of expansion of the blogosphere—4,500,000 blogs as of November 2004, and an expected doubling in 2005—you can expect the blogosphere to infringe upon your life or organization in the future, perhaps the immediate future.

Still not convinced? Then ask yourself if you care about the media—*in any way whatsoever*. Do you read the papers with an eye on how your organization is dealt with? Do you check to see if your ads are running where you thought they were going to run? Do you scan for news about your market area, your customer type, demographic info, or anything whatsoever?

If you do, then you must develop a blog strategy, beginning with the defensive moves, because the blogosphere *is* the media. Go back to chapter 4 and read the stats on the crumbling of the audience for MSM. That audience is moving rapidly into the blogosphere. The blogosphere is an information universe just like the television networks, the newspapers, and talk radio. People are acting on the information provided there. If you care about anything in media, then you must care about the blogosphere.

If you have a vice president of communications or some such person designated in some such position, ask for his or her opinion on the blogosphere. It is the first step to understanding where you are in relation to the threat. Imagine asking the director of facilities at the Los Angeles Unified School District for his opinion on earthquake preparedness and getting back a blank look. If your veep for communications says, "Blogosphere? What's that?" you have the same problem as the LAUSD superintendent. Would that superintendent walk away without taking action? Will you?

First, find out if you are already a subject for discussion and reporting in the blogosphere. There are a number of search engines that can help you in this regard, including **Technorati** and **Daypop** (**daypop.com**). Task a team of cyber-savvy types—*from across the organization*—to conduct the hunt. Bonus the man or woman who brings back the most complete report. The blogosphere thrives on such competition, so use a competition to chart your present position. If you are too small to have such resources, tap a few mid-level bloggers to consult with you. If you are GM, hire David Sifry from Technorati—good enough for CNN, good enough for you.

EXAMPLE: You are the largest car dealer in Cleveland. You

need a report on blogs that deal with cars, blogs that deal with your makes and models, blogs that deal with auto repair, and of course blogs that deal with Cleveland generally, consumer protection in Cleveland specifically, and any blog that has ever mentioned you, your business, or your employees. With that in hand you will at least have a map of the blogosphere's geography pertinent to you.

EXAMPLE: You are the pastor of a megachurch in Phoenix. You should already know about George Barna's website with the latest polling data on the church in America, and of course you will know and visit Rick Warren's **Pastors.com**. (If you are unaware of Warren, his book *The Purpose Driven Life* has sold twenty million copies in three years.) But what about the blogs? Are you reading **Mark D. Roberts** and **Evangelical Outpost** and **Al Mohler** at **Crosswalk.com** and Biola University's John Mark Reynolds's blog? That's just a start. Ask some congregants to get you up to speed. Convene a study session and round-table on the issue. Get smart, now.

EXAMPLE: You are a senior exec at Nordstrom. They have an internet team there, so you assume they are working on this. Call over and ask for a blog status report. If they don't have one, do the research and write one for them, or send everyone there (and as appropriate, folks in the chain of command) a copy of this book. Put a Post-It note on this page.

You should now be committed to developing and implementing the components of a defensive strategy for the blogosphere. This strategy will have at least three key elements.

1. A CHAIN OF COMMAND

Who is in charge of a blog storm? When and if you or your organization attracts the attention of one or one thousand blogs, you will have to move quickly to respond. Who's got the authority to do so?

2. An Organization Policy on Blogs by Employees

In an interview I did with Chairman of the Joint Chiefs of Staff General Richard Myers, I asked him if he read the milblogs— specifically those blogs by active duty and reservist Army, Navy, Air Force, and Marine Corps personnel. He said he didn't but that he knew he had to find time to do so. I asked Karl Rove, assistant to President Bush and political guru, if he read the blogs. He said no but that he had set up a system to keep him informed of what they were saying.

The *Sacramento Bee*'s best political columnist, Dan Weintraub, launched a hugely successful blog during California's tumultuous recall election of 2003, but there was controversy over a Weintraub posting, and suddenly his posts had to be submitted for review prior to posting—a policy developed on the fly and a lousy one at that.

You need to think through and articulate a clear policy on the subject and then stick with it, changing it only after due consideration. I think attempts to ban employee blogging will prove impossible, so it's best to put out guidelines on the use of company information, best practices, and a warning on what sort of blogging behavior can get you canned.

3. Transparency

If and when the blog swarm arrives, deal with it in exactly the opposite fashion from how CBS did during Ra^thergate. Don't hunker down. Don't insult the swarm members. Put a premium on disclosure of facts that can be disclosed and the transparency of your response. Engage senior leadership and put its members on the record.

And crucially, admit error as soon as error is evident to you. If in good faith you don't believe there is error, declare why and repeatedly defend your position with patience, humility, and have a line of retreat open if needed.

During the height of the internet boom, Doonesbury ran a series of hilarious cartoons on the presence within internet companies of "seers": gurus, big thinkers, "over-the-horizon" types. The lampooning was fun, but as to the blogs, guess what? You need a seer or two. Start with Clark Judge at the White House Writers Group or Professor Glenn Reynolds, or the **PowerLine** guys. Bring them in. Blue-sky it.

But get started. Don't ask your consultants for other matters to run with this ball either, unless they know right away what you are talking about.

The earthquake may never happen. The hurricane may never arrive. But if either does, you will be glad you built to code.

EXPLOITING THE NEW MEDIUM

Getting in Touch with
Your Inner Blog

I'll bet your organization has a mission statement, right? Most organizations do, and in fact they spent lots of time, effort, and usually money to develop them. Core values and all that.

And probably most of your employees/organization members can find it if they have to, but they don't carry it around in their heads. Congratulations to you on establishing and maintaining an excellent corporate culture if they do, but don't fool yourself. There's a lot going on every day. It is hard to keep the mission in mind when a shipment is lost, a deadline passed, or a hysterical spouse on the phone because one of your kids totaled the car.

Maintaining focus on key goals is tough stuff. That's one of the key missions of any internal communications system. But who has the time to really manage that? What starts out to be a means of staying in touch with an organization becomes a chronically late, vanilla newsletter with a list of birthdays and "years served" milestones mixed in with a staff-generated "Message from the President" on the achievements of six months ago.

It doesn't have to be that way. But only leadership can change it.

LEADERSHIP BLOGGING

If you are a leader, then you ought to be blogging, and the folks you lead ought to be reading that blog.

Every day, if possible. Most days, if not.

Eisner should be blogging for Disney. Rumsfeld for the Pentagon. Martha from the federal facility in which she presently sits and from the boardroom when she returns. Jennings for *ABC News*, Katie for *The Today Show* staff, editor Marty Baron for the *Boston Globe*.

The CEOs of GM, Ford, and Chrysler-Daimler should be dictating or typing their entries daily. So should the heads of mutual funds and studios, snack kings, airline princes, and the royalty of fashion empires. While they should be always aware that the text can be cut and pasted and shipped to the world, that risk shouldn't paralyze executives with leadership responsibilities.

Every single day a blog gives talented executives an opportunity to communicate with their troops: to inspire, inform, cajole, or plead. Mostly to inform. In the first person, it will be read. It will do everything the newsletter can't because it is authentically your voice.

If you build it, they will come. Really. If you figure out how to blog effectively—find a voice and use it—your organization's productivity will soar. If you take feedback, you'll actually know what's going on. Those management levels vanish in the medium of blogging. You'll hear about the doofus who is a petty tyrant, and if you set the example of encouragement and praise, you'll hear about the superstars and the folks who went the extra mile.

EXAMPLE: After three months of blogging and figuring out how to work the machinery and finding a voice, say Bruce Bright, CEO of ReallyBigCompany, begins his morning blog this way:

> Before we get caught up in end-of-year inventory, I'd like to take a moment to thank James Jones, Sarah Smith, and Archie Young. Their manager, Joe Grounds, sent me an e-mail that these three spent their weekend here, churning out the report we needed to provide the compliance manager at CalOSHA. Without that report, we'd have gotten some dings for lateness. Instead we are on time, our report is professional and complete, and we can report that we had no injuries at the Jackson plant for the fourth year in a row. This stuff counts. You did a great job, James, Sarah, and Archie—and you, too, Joe. I checked. I understand you were here with them. Thanks to you all.

What would the effect of such a post be, when viewed by ReallyBigCompany's four thousand employees? The named quartet would get relentless teasing for a day, and they would love Bruce Bright forever. Others would take note that Bright was taking note of effort. Managers would get the idea that their efforts are appreciated as well. Everybody would win.

Of course an idiot with a blog could destroy a company's morale and probably invite defamation suits by the hundreds and intentional-infliction-of-emotional-distress suits by the scores. But idiots aren't generally CEOs, and if they are, they'll bring the company down eventually anyway. If you are a leader who has ever complained about the inability to communicate effectively or in a timely fashion with your people, there is no excuse for delay. Start a leadership blog today.

MANAGEMENT BLOGGING

So your job isn't to inspire or lead. You are a manager. You have goals to meet and outputs to measure. You have folks below you and folks above you. In fact, you have a lot of folks above you, some of whom wouldn't mind getting you out the door. You have folks below you who would love to take your place. How does a blog serve you?

First, if you need to communicate with your team, you can do so most easily with a blog that sticks to the most basic of messages and the most simple of commands. Risk-averse? Then limit your posts to the sort of information that everyone really needs and always seems to misplace: Approved vendors. The contact list at the key clients. Office directory.

Some will argue that there are no "basic messages," no information that can be shared out. "The contacts at key clients," they'll say. "Are you nuts? Our competitors get ahold of that and they'll be dialing immediately. We could lose the account!"

Perhaps. But that sort of response is a red flare—an admission that your relationship with a client is in the most vulnerable of all situations: a connection that can be severed by a simple phone call. In an age of rushing information, sequestering your code isn't exactly a sound strategy.

It is important to assume that everything posted will be read by everyone. But even with that excellent caution in the back of your mind, the blog you start can be the blog that draws the attention of the senior management and wins the loyalty and extra effort of the employees or members downstream.

EMPLOYEE BLOGGING

Post a nasty entry about the boss, and you will get fired. Post a shallow bit of flattery, and you will earn scorn. Post suggestions that require harder work from lazy colleagues, and you will earn their enmity.

So, is there any upside to blogging?

Yes, but not about people or structures within the company—at least, not usually. But gather useful information about competitors, or link to valuable websites/articles, and you will gain the grudging admiration of your colleagues and higher-ups, and perhaps the attention of folks in other places who will pay you more to do a more interesting job.

But if you attack or gossip or complain, you will find your blog was a quick exit to the door. And rightly so.

Which raises the question: ought organizations to oblige their members to blog as a means of quickly assessing talents/flaws? It is impossible to keep up appearances of professional competence when under the microscope, and there is no better microscope than a blog. High-risk strategy, but potentially useful in some settings, especially hyper-competitive ones.

BLOGGING YOU, YOUR PRODUCT, OR YOUR ORGANIZATION TO THE WORLD

Who are you? Do you want the world to know? What are you selling? Do you want to sell much, much more?

Some folks want the world to know what they think—they themselves, not their PR department, not their corporate communications consultant, just them. They value their own opinions and believe these opinions have value for others. The 4,500,000-plus bloggers out there are among that number.

Barbra Streisand is a blogger. A not-very-bright one, but a blogger nonetheless. She hasn't been right on politics ever, as far as I can tell, but she has the confidence of immense theatrical, singing, and directorial talent, which she wrongly believes translates into wisdom in areas outside her expertise.

So she occasionally lets fly with a screed at her website, **BarbraStreisand.com.** On those days my job as a talk-show host is easier. And for those who look to Barbra for guidance and inspiration, they get their dose of Babs.

I'd like to read a blog by Harvard's president, Lawrence H.

Summers. He's a smart guy, well read, wrestling with this enormous institution with its billions and billions of assets both financial and intellectual. What's he got to say about this and that?

Or Rudy. What's Rudy up to most days? The man can obviously think on his feet. As can Arnold. And Zell. Anyone you know by his or her first name should be blogging.

Yes, there are risks, especially for public figures, but we overestimate those risks in an age as forgiving of blunders as ours is. The doomsayers warn that text will be taken out of context and used to attack. Of course it will, but in an information-savvy age, there is almost instant immunity if the target is being attacked with text rather than audio or video. Text that is free of hate or profanity can rarely harm.

But text can do wonders for reputation and following. Demonstrate skill and thought, and you'll attract a crowd and then a following. If you can use either, get started.

And anyone who is trying to sell anything can use both.

Blogging is a nearly cost-free opportunity to establish or defend a brand and to introduce new products or buzz, and to do so over and over again. If Glenn Reynolds—the **Instapundit**, remember, with the biggest traffic on the web—if Glenn likes your new digital camera and writes about it, you have a home run. What if you were a blogger with Glenn's audience size? You could have plugged your own digital camera.

My last book made the *New York Times* bestsellers list for four or five consecutive weeks following its publication on July 10, 2004, peaking at number sixteen. The only print advertising it received occurred after it had peaked. It did benefit from my relentless plugging of it on my radio show—"If you don't tell them, nobody will" is another bit of coach talk from my pal Tardie—but its initial success was because of blog buzz: thousands and thousands of free encounters with potential purchasers mediated through friendly notices in the poliblogs. Imagine being given free ads in all the small papers of America and a few of the bigs. That's what the blogosphere did for my book.

That's what the blogosphere can do for your product, reputation, or organization as well, first on your own blog. Go to **Hugh Hewitt** right now and you'll see that I am flogging this book, *Blog*, even as you read it. But run a **Technorati** search of **Hugh Hewitt** and you'll also see that the blogosphere is once again raining attention on the book (not all of it kind, of course).

Dedication to blogging will establish a reputation on the internet much more quickly than you can imagine, especially if supported by genuine reciprocity and other media.

EXAMPLE: The release date for *Blockbuster X* is ten months out. The director has never blogged a single entry. So the studio execs sit him down for a day, train him, and assign him a ghost if necessary. DirectorsCutBlog appears the next day, and it is supported via blog ads, ads in the trades, and some careful orchestration by the folks at GraceHill, who have been patiently establishing good relations with uber-bloggers for the past three years. Before long, because the director is a pretty talented, verbal fellow, he's got a few thousand visitors a day. The week before the release he conducts an online conversation with critics, the first of its kind prior to the release of the film. He also maintains an online diary of the rollout. Finally, he starts posting the reviews and reviewing the reviews.

He's the first to do it and generates huge buzz as a result. Before long, a dozen copycats surface, which is fine, since all blogs are copycats, and the public thirst for info is limitless. The gatekeepers at the Calendar section of the *Los Angeles Times* or *Variety* no longer get to mediate the decisions on which directors get profiled, which movies get reviewed, which publicist gets favored treatment. All of sudden it is about the talent.

EXAMPLE: You are a young realtor in a hyper-competitive market. Your competitors have been putting up open-house signs for twenty years and have a stable of clients that have bought many houses from them. You can climb the ladder the old-fashioned way, by holding open houses for other agents, dropping leaflets by the thousands, or buying ads in the local weekly paper.

Or you can buy the local BuyAHomeBlog.com franchise and begin to instantly inform the universe of home hunters in your city about what's new on the market and its price and features, then offer to show it to them at their convenience ("Just send an e-mail or call!"). You continue to do the traditional marketing, but now you are including your blog in every print piece and on every card. It isn't a website—websites are too static and clunky. It is you doing your marketing by serving the immediate information needs of home buyers. You don't try to control the client by parceling out info; you trust the info-hungry purchaser to reward you for your information, at least enough of the time to make it worth your while.

The crucial difference between websites and blogs is the authentic voice and earned credibility. Websites aren't going anywhere. They are part of the information explosion, but the difference between a blog with credibility and a website is the difference between an ad in the fourth section of the local paper and a conversation with that paper's editor about which neighborhood to buy in or which movie to see.

MARKETING THROUGH THE BLOGOSPHERE: BUYING THE EYEBALLS

Let's talk about blog ads first.

These are the right-margin (sometimes left-margin) ads that

appear on websites with traffic and some without. The pricing is left to the website owner, and the blog-ad people take a cut. Right now the pricing is ludicrously low because Glenn Reynolds at **Instapundit** sets the market in the way that JetBlue sets the market for coast-to-coast travel from around the area of Long Beach. If you can have Glenn's traffic for Glenn's price, why not buy that? When Glenn gets around to pushing the ceiling, Weimar-like inflation will hit the blog-ad world.

For a period of time I experimented with super-pricing of blog ads, setting a rate in the summer of 2004 far above Glenn's even though my traffic was less than half of his, with rates of $1,000, $1,500, and $3,000 for one-week, two-week, or one-month runs respectively. I sold only two ads, one of which I declined because its content was inappropriate to my audience. But I did prove to myself that there are some ad buyers out there who have issued "Buy the top blogs" orders without much attention to pricing. Then I adjusted my pricing to Glenn's and will now follow his cues using my traffic as a percentage of his traffic to set my ads. (Glenn: Raise your rates—they are ridiculously low.)

Why tell you this? Because blog ads are among the most effective and inexpensive ads in the world to reach high-income and/or high-intelligence audiences with instant follow-up. Say you are a Saab dealer. Don't you want Saab HQ to be on every major blog with a click-through ad to a listing of all of Saab's new models, their wonderful qualities, and a listing of dealers by geography? If you don't, you don't know your audience.

Trying to sell a high-end book? A small ad in the *New York Times Review of Books* will get a fleeting bit of attention from a few million eyeballs, but a blog ad running across twenty major blogs for a week will cost less and present far more specific info; it can also be linked directly to the **Amazon.com** page.

Do you cater to enthusiasts of one sort or another, from fly-fishing to adventure travel? Find the blogs that already own that space, buy out their inventory, and possibly hire the owner. Sponsorship has risks to the authenticity of the voice and thus the trust factor, but it bears investigating.

Crucially, the pricing structure of the blog-ad world will change quickly in response to this book and others like it. The efficiency of the buy is too great. So speed is of the essence. Locking down long-term deals now with budding bloggers of promise and rising reputations is a key strategy. Ask your ad buyers for suggestions. If they don't have any, find new ad buyers. That's like telling a soap producer in the late forties that television would never make it.

Of course, the smart executives will immediately figure out that blog ads are the best way going to narrowcast for an audience. Say you are selling Pampers. If there is a NewMomBlog out there with traffic in the hundreds of thousands every day, would you rather get a blog ad with a coupon up and running there for a couple of hundred (or thousand) bucks a month, or scattershot to the world in the Sunday papers? Focus-group a hundred new moms. Find out who reads the blogs. Take them into a separate room and make a list. Buy all the blog ads you can on long-term contracts for those blogs. You win.

Say for whatever reason you want to reach young evangelical men between the ages of eighteen and thirty. Who would want to do so? Well, seminary admissions officers for one, about twenty publishers for another.

If that's your target, get in touch with **Stones Cry Out** (**stones-cry-out.blogspot.com**), **Matt Crash** (**mattcrash.blogs pot.com**), and **GotDesign** (**gotdesign.blogspot.com**), three hot young evangelical bloggers, plus **Evangelical Outpost, Mark D.**

Roberts, **John Mark Reynolds**, **Al Mohler**, and a bunch of other **Blogs4God** traffic kings, and you have penetrated deep into your target market.

The list is endless, and the blog ads offer visual opportunities plus a click-through potential to specific products that will quickly run rings around old media.

Now here's the revolutionary marketing concept: Build your own blog that attracts an audience and own the blog-ad strip for yourself forever. Don't just buy blog ads from NewMomBlog if you sell Pampers—start NewMomBlog or its equivalent.

Do you get it yet? You can own the television network rather than just buy Super Bowl ads once a year. Look at the traffic trajectory! Don't live in the electronic cave that the networks hope you never leave. Information acquisition habits are changing. Build the places where the customer wants to go, and market to him or her once he or she gets there.

This potential has applicability beyond consumer products. If you are one of those issue advertisers out there who need occasionally to move Congress or the state legislatures in one direction or another, wouldn't it be great to own the most interesting blog in each state capital and to be able to program the blog ads with suggested actions vis-à-vis important bills even as your commentators attract traffic because they are the best writers/reporters on what's going on in Sacramento, Columbus, or D.C.? If you, your company, or your trade group has ever attempted to influence even a single legislative vote or administrative agency action, then you need to get a blog going that will be a grassroots organizing tool when the need arises.

In a later chapter I will tell you how to find the bloggers you need. Keep in mind you don't much care about the content provided it (1) brings traffic that can also sample your blog ad and (2) isn't a countermessage if you have a message.

MARKETING THROUGH THE BLOGOSPHERE: EARNING THE EYEBALLS

You probably already know the difference between *paid media* and *earned media*. Paid media is what you buy and control the content of: commercials on television and radio, print advertising, direct mail, billboards, and the blog ads just discussed.

Earned media is the attention of the media that you earn by doing what you do. Bring out a great new car, and automobile writers/magazines will cover it for free because their readers expect them to. Bring out a bestseller, and I'll interview you on the radio show for free because you are of interest to my audience. Running for office? You can buy a flight of ads and no doubt will, but interviews or favorable coverage has to be earned.

You can earn the attention of the blogosphere, but it requires a lot of sophistication that begins with the essential understanding of the new media: Except for a handful of bloggers whose reputation wasn't founded on the fact that they blog, bloggers are very sensitive to commentary about them or their blogs. This is because it is their passport to attention and possibly income. Blast a blogger, and you may be striking at his lifeline. Compliment a blogger, and the favor will be remembered for a very long time.

As an undergrad at Harvard almost thirty years ago, I went to a talk by an author who had written a biography of William Loeb, the then-legendary publisher of the *Manchester Union Leader*. The author, whose name I have forgotten, made a remark that I have never forgotten: Write a biography of a living person, he said, and you are assured of selling at least one copy. It may not have been original to him, but it sure made sense. It continues to make sense every day. Write about a blog and that blogger will eventually learn of your comment, usually in pretty quick fashion.

All blogs are written to be read, and the evidence of reading is traffic and subsequent reaction. When I link to another blog from **Hugh Hewitt,** I almost always get a thank-you from that blogger as it sends traffic to him. A link from Glenn Reynolds's **Instapundit**—yes, him again—had so great an effect on traffic that it coined a term the "Instalanche," which meant the spike in visitors that followed a Glenn mention. When my blog began to generate the same, the spike was called by some the "Hughicane." Other terms will arise as blog traffic flows from different sources.

There are many words for the effects of a link from the **Drudge Report (drudgereport.com)** or a mention from Rush, by the way—including *server crash* and *unexpected bandwidth charges.* So powerful have these two new media gatekeepers become that an urgent word from one or the other can send websites over the cliff in a minute or two. But still it is the greatest thing in the world for a blogger: the equivalent of an author getting a call from Oprah announcing an invitation to appear and have his book join the club.

So understand that bloggers love traffic, and they are sensitive about their reputations as bloggers. There is one more thing: they are very easily co-opted. All it requires is genuine appreciation for genuine talent.

Not that they are different in this way from any other journalists, or indeed any other performers. Journalists of all sorts, just like actors and writers and performers from the beginning of recorded history, live for the reviews. "You like me, you really like me!" blurted a joyous Sally Fields, in one of the most authentic moments in the history of the Academy Awards. There was never an honest author who didn't care what the readers and critics thought, nor an honest actor indifferent to the reviews.

Reporters want Pulitzers and television producers and

anchors want Emmys and Peabodys just as the movie types want Oscars. If they can't have those things, they'll settle for anything else that comes with status attached. And lacking status, they'll take genuine praise. No genuine praise? Well, flattery will do for some, though not for all.

It is the rare individual—a second-term president who doesn't care who his successor is, perhaps, or a pope at the end of his life—who can be indifferent to the media. That doesn't mean never making an enemy or sending out sharp words. Enemies and sharp words are the inevitable by-products of public significance.

But it doesn't hurt to have lots of friends who deal in print and airtime, whether on the radio or on the tube.

And increasingly it doesn't hurt to have friends in the blogosphere. The enemies will find you even if you don't go looking, but friends are a different thing entirely.

So how to go about making friends in the blogosphere? Here are some specific steps.

First, acquaint yourself with the form, and having done so, decide who genuinely does a good job, who meets your information needs. Then tell them. Via e-mail. Repeatedly. Bloggers live by e-mail from people they have never met. They may not write back, but most spend a lot of time reading their e-mails. I do. Every blogger I know does. I don't bother responding to the nuts, and there are lots and lots of nuts. Or the haters. But I do try to stay in touch with the diligent, and always with the valuable sources who provide me leads and neat data. So be of help to key bloggers, and they will be of help to you.

Next, do what studios do when studios want movie critics to notice their wares: Throw a junket! I speculated long ago that the first Las Vegas casino to figure this out and host a blogger convention with comped rooms will get millions of dollars in free publicity and begin a tradition that will grow and grow as the years go by. If it throws in an awards ceremony inaugurating the first ever "Instys" awards, blogging's Pulitzers will be established (assuming the judging is done by reputable bloggers who agree that they cannot consider themselves eligible).

It isn't just Vegas that can collect on the universal human desire for free stuff and its companion lust for recognition. Silicon Valley can honor high-tech bloggers; Detroit can gather car bloggers; you get the picture. Be good to the bloggers, and they will be good to you.

Put bloggers on your advisory boards if you are a university or a college, and maybe on your board of directors if you are a consumer-products company that doesn't want to get left behind. Pay bloggers to consult, or ask your consultants to blog. But don't ignore the phenomenon in the early stages where your investment of attention, time, and money can bring huge rewards.

FINDING A BLOGGER FOR YOUR ORGANIZATION'S BLOG

So I have persuaded you that your organization needs a blog. Who to ask to man it?

The best bloggers have self-selected themselves already. Spend a week on the web, following your nose, zipping from site to site. Ignore design. Ignore color. Find who can write and who is ridiculously productive. One of the reasons old media hates new media so much is that new media is so much more productive than old media. Every day bloggers churn out postings by the hundreds of thousands, and some of us will post a dozen times a day, each one of which is worth reading.

We are wired this way. We are good with words. Our brains race. We can't—most of us, at least—golf. But we are scratch handicappers when it comes to idea discovery and manipulation. Most of the best can turn a phrase.

Find five bloggers you like, preferably with medium-traffic scores—not high, unless you have big bucks, and not so low as to fail a hurdle that must be passed every day. Send the five—or twenty-five if you are Coke or GM—an e-mail offering them employment as a blogger. Ask them to name the price. Choose three. Tell them to start thinking about serving your need, which is . . .

You have begun. No meetings. No endless grinding down of the creative spark by committees of golfers.

It is that simple. The talent pool is on display every day. No executive search firm is necessary. Start three prototypes and run them internally for a month. Pick the best, or if they don't work, start over. Get good confidentiality agreements at the start, and part company on good terms with any blogger who leaves. It isn't hard to figure this out.

Don't let the lawyers kill the idea. They'll want to. Ask them for all the cases involving lawsuits that were prompted by blogging. Right—not many if any.

One more thing that applies if you are considering blogging as part of a medium- or large-sized company: send an e-mail to all hands and ask any bloggers in the organization to come to a virtual meeting conducted on the web, where the idea of how blogging affects or could affect your company will be debated via serial posting. Offer anonymity if desired.

You might already have a superstar blogger in your midst.

THERE IS PLENTY OF TIME TO START

I had never met UCLA Law Professor Stephen Bainbridge and his wife when my wife and I were brought together with them at a dinner party with two other wonderful couples. Across the table we talked blogging, and Professor Bainbridge sighed that it was too late to jump into the pool even though he was interested. I chided his response, and effectively so. Not long thereafter he began **ProfessorBainbridge.com**, and his readership has soared. He blogs on corporate securities law, wine, and politics. He's a go-to guy on Martha Stewart, California cabernets, and scores of other topics.

Because millions of people have not even begun to use the internet, much less formed their habits when it comes to blog selection, the competition has barely begun for mindspace and blogroll links. The key is beginning and then paying attention to posting and interesting links. Specific steps follow, but there is practically no reason not to begin.

I advised this course in my 2003 book *In, But Not Of: A Guide* to *Christian Ambition and the Desire to Influence the World*. I advised it in my 2004 book, *If It's Not Close, They Can't Cheat: Crushing the Democrats in Every Election and Why Your Life Depends on It*. (Those chapters are included in Appendix A, as are my other columns on blogging and the new media.) Many people have followed that advice, and, as mentioned above, there are now more than one hundred blogs that credit me with giving them a push into blogging.

They all have readers, and they all are virtually indestructible records of opinions and change. Each has an impact, and many have great impacts. More will follow and each will, in turn, encourage others. The dynamic is the dynamic of the Reformation, where individual encouraged individual to discover truth and propagate it.

Success is difficult to define in the blogosphere because it is both intangible and fleeting. If the president of the United States reads your blog, is that enough even though it is only one reader?

If your son or daughter does, now or in fifty years, is that enough?

If you help topple Dan Rather or help elect John Thune in South Dakota or Richard Burr in North Carolina, thus changing the course of history in the United States, is that enough?

Or if you implement a blog strategy that bears fruit when the crisis comes for your company but you are thus positioned to stay ahead of the news curve and on top of the story, will that be enough?

Or if you transform your newspaper or your radio station before the market deserts you, will that be enough?

If you network your congregation via your blog so they know your thoughts on a variety of subjects and more deeply integrate themselves into the life of your church, is that enough?

If you serve your fans by sharing with them the creative process, provide the occasional essay for free, or point twenty people toward your favorite bed-and-breakfast so that they, too, can enjoy it, are any of those things enough?

Or if you sell a million more packages of Pampers than you would have had you ignored the blogosphere, would that be enough?

The point is that all of these results and more—vastly more—are available to you. But you do have to start.

A DOZEN BLOGS I WOULD
LAUNCH IF I WERE . . .

Because blogs are a category of internet site with a unique voice that earns the trust of readers, thus causing the readers to return again and again for information, everything that has enthusiasts can have blogs, from butterflies to postage stamps to theology to aircraft carriers. If there are websites already devoted to a subject area, then blogs are out there as well, or coming soon. Every niche is an opportunity to become a blog entrepreneur, anticipating the rise of blog-ad revenue and deciding to build the blog that will have the traffic that produces the revenue, or to corner the blog market for the business you are already in. Thus, here are some examples of what I would do if I were . . .

A PUBLISHER

Imagine BookManBlog, a sprightly written, Amazon-linked, continually updated blog on the publishing world. The author reads continually from all the book reviews that appear online and links to the ones he approves of. Because BookManBlog generates buzz in the industry, publishers vie to buy space from his blog-ad allocation despite the enormous cost. When BookMan fingers a title, its sales soar. Oprah reads BookMan. So does every book-review editor in America. Every best-seller list available electronically is there, as well as stock prices of the major houses and new release lists. It is an author's and agent's paradise or inferno.

BookMan doesn't rule the publishing world, but he gets invited to all of its parties. He doesn't represent authors, but he's asked by agents for his contact list. Bookstore owners with inventory issues send him e-mails. Fans ask for his opinion on this or that title. Joseph Epstein compares him to Samuel Johnson.

There is presently no such site and no such BookMan, but with a day's thought and phone calls, the biggest publishers should try to establish such a site and to immediately begin to build traffic to it via a variety of marketing tools. It's a race. There can be more than one winner, just as every season of television brings more than one success.

But the gun has already gone off.

A MUSICIAN

MusicianBlog would collect all the links to music resources that are commonly used, plus links to the online editions of magazines for musicians and music enthusiasts. It would include a link to Amazon's CD checkout, of course, and a comprehensive listing of recording studios and performance schedules by region.

But its heart and soul would be three or four music critics contributing the latest buzz on the various spheres, whether opera or reggae, rock or chamber music. With decent design, it could become a crossroads for thousands of performers who need info on medical benefits and easy gigs, short-term rentals and the business of cruise-line lounges. All in one place, with classifieds.

AN EBAY ENTREPRENEUR

Chairman of the House Rules Committee David Dreier is a weekly guest on my radio program, and he often talks about how the new economy is difficult to measure given the appearance of so many new professions. "There are 40,000 people making a full-time living on Ebay," he often declares, "and the jobs report doesn't count them!"

Do they have a blog voice yet—or two or three? Would **EbayBlog** attract these 40,000 for news and views on the business of being a middleman? Would the space have value as a means of sharing out the secrets of efficiency and marketing? Of course.

GENERAL MOTORS

The name **GMBlog.com** is reserved, but by whom? For what purpose? The folks at the top of GM ought to be worried about that.

A FISHERMAN

I have been fishing twice. Once with my gramps when I was four or five, and once with Terry Tuma. Said **WalleyeCentral.com** about Terry:

> Terry Tuma, affectionately known as "Tackle Terry" is a multi-species angler whose articles have appeared in virtually all the

top fishing publications in the Midwest. He is a dynamic speaker who can convey the fun of fishing to audiences of all ages and skill levels. As one outdoor writer said of him, "He can stop crappies with a wave of the rod. He can catch sunfish with hypnotic powers." Terry's seminars on bluegills and crappies ought to be interesting!

I caught a twenty-pound pike on my frolic with Terry, an event that ought to have been recorded on Terry's blog. Named **FishermanBlog.com**, it's a place for anglers to gather and exchange stories via a comments section, while Terry clipped coupons from the blog-ads column on the right margin. Terry, if you are reading this, I reserved the name. It is yours for free if you tell folks about my twenty-pound pike.

ANY FORTUNE 500 COMPANY

You ought to own the name of your company followed by *blog*, as in DowJonesBlog or Johnson&JohnsonBlog. You should be using it to spread whatever message you want to spread about your company. It may be a leadership blog—see the earlier chapter— or a lobbying blog—see the conclusion after that—but you should own it.

A CLEVELAND BROWNS FAN

Or any fan of any sports team, really. If it's a team that floats your boat, grab the space and declare your authority. What's a differing voice going to do, fire you? BrownsBlog.com or DawgPound Blog.com will draw traffic away from the official and sanitized sites where combustibility is often frowned upon. Then there's the niche of the NFL draft. Start NFLDraftBlog.com and Mel Kiper will be bidding to buy the name from you. Or ESPN. But don't sell. Keep it and update it, and watch your traffic begin to rise early every February when the hot-stove league takes off. Wherever there are enthusiasts, there are blog niches waiting to happen.

A UNIVERSITY OF MICHIGAN LAW SCHOOL GRAD

Yeah, I have reserved **UMLawBlog.com**. I'll give it to the school when they figure out that they need the dean to post daily.

Lawyers and law profs have done very well in the blogo-sphere, because they have already developed the habits of research and exposition that make for interesting posts. Eugene Volokh is a sort of mad-scientist-libertarian-First-Amendment-law-prof who started **The Volokh Conspiracy** a few years ago. Its popularity has fallen as Eugene diluted the brand by inviting oth-ers to post at the site, but it is an experimental site that EV must see as pushing the margins of the blogosphere out.

Other lawblogs such as **How Appealing** (**legalaffairs.org/howappealing**) and **BeldarBlog** have filled the law side of the blogosphere, and more will arrive. When the first Supreme Court nominee of the new media era arrives, watch the blogs explode with commentary and investigation. Every opinion the nominee wrote or case on which the nominee participated will serve as fodder for the new media. Anita Hill would not have lasted a weekend with the new media on her case. But a flawed nominee will melt more quickly than a Popsicle in Vegas in July. When that nominee is announced, check **nomineeblog.com** or **Supreme Court Blog** (**scotus.blogspot.com**). And **PowerLine** as well. It will be a magnificent battle of text merchants.

A RUNNER

I have been putting the miles down since 1979, and after a half-dozen Marine Corps Marathons and an assortment of others, a few injuries, and a spouse's struggle with plantar fasciitis, I'd love to find a blog that captured the spirit of George Sheehan, a *Runner's World* legend whose columns helped spark the first running boom of the late seventies and early eighties. Sheehan would have been a blogger, and the fact that there is a website, **GeorgeSheehan.com**, proves as much. There's another Sheehan out there waiting to provide a daily journal of the love-hate addiction that is long-distance running by amateurs.

THE MANAGER OF ANY CONCERT VENUE

Behind the scenes is a place most people would love to go, and every venue manager can take them there, and while giving them a glimpse of Rod Stewart or the Dixie Chicks, could also be selling them tickets to the next event. Building a community around a venue should be among the easier marketing efforts, but only if the boss really is involved and really does open the window on what's going on inside.

As you can see, this list could go on endlessly. The blogosphere awaits you. Get started.

13

GETTING STARTED: THE TECHNOLOGY

I am so unqualified to write about technology that anyone who knows me is laughing as he or she reads this chapter heading. Which is why you should really be convinced that being a techno-phobe is no barrier to blogging.

I learned how to spell-check in September of 2004. I had been blogging for more than two years by that point.

I still can't use a digital camera, but my blog had 160,000 vis-itors in the twenty-four-hour period surrounding the October 8, 2004, presidential debate and a quarter-million visitors during the forty-eight hours before, during, and after the November 2 voting.

Design-savvy bloggers mock my layout, and rightly so. At a party thrown by **Lileks** at Jasperwood, following a tour of his Hummels room and the drinking of much fine single-malt scotch, the assembled bloggers turned on me as if one and conducted a blogging intervention devoted to telling me how much **Hugh Hewitt** sucks. Sure the traffic was off the charts, but couldn't I get an RSS feed? I am still unsure what an RSS feed is and have trouble making the permalinks work—*but it does not matter*! That's the point.

It is all about the content.

So, if you are interested, go to **typepad.com, blogger.com, blogspot.com,** or any of the many other services out there and discover how easy it is to begin, even if you are a two-finger typist who can't get the garage door to go up. Visit many blogs and see which ones you like, then go with the service they used. Look at the costs. Success means bandwidth charges.

I don't really know what that means, but I think it means that the more traffic you get, the more the servers have to spin or do whatever it is they do, and you get charged more. Most bloggers pay a few bucks a month. Successful ones pay a couple hundred. Blog-ad revenue will almost surely catch up with traffic costs. My radio producer, Duane, who operates **radioblogger.com**, achieved profitability in sixty days. It helps to have radio plugs, of course, but it really isn't hard to keep costs low, certainly less than even a moderate golfing jones.

The key rules of blogging success and significance are these:

- Post often.
- Link freely.
- Be generous in praise and attribution.
- Don't be long-winded too often, if at all. Brevity is the soul of blogging when you are getting started.
- Paragraphs are your friend.
- Profanity loses audiences.
- Avoid feuds and flame wars.
- At least at the start, skip the comments sections. You end up with the problem of nuts if you are any good.
- Keep the title short and easy to remember so that it is

easy to recall and type into the space at the top of the page.

Joe Carter at **Evangelical Outpost** has a series on getting started that is invaluable, and **Stones Cry Out** posted last fall on the role of low—or moderate-traffic bloggers. Read both sites extensively. In fact, read them every day as well as the high-traffic blogs that make the weather.

There is more start-up advice in the chapters from my earlier books, which, again, are reproduced in Appendix A.

CONCLUSION

THE INEVITABILITY OF DOMINANCE

As the presidential campaign crescendoed this past fall, the blog traffic exploded as political junkies and ordinary Americans trolled the poliblogs for news of any sort. The appetite was extraordinary, and clearinghouse websites such as **RealClear Politics**—in essence a blog run by two very smart information entrepreneurs, John McIntyre and Tom Bevin—became jumping-off springboards into the world of the blogs. *Time, Newsweek, The Wall Street Journal,* and all the major newspapers began tracking the commentary and news reporting on the blogs, as eager as the general public for indicators of surfacing stories or momentum shifts.

This was as it will be for a very long time to come. Blogs are built on speed and trust, and MSM is very slow and very distrusted. This is especially true when it comes to political news and even reporting on the Global War on Terror. It is especially true among certain demographics that include political conservatives and people for whom faith is a huge component of their lives. It will become increasingly true for everyone in the entertainment and publishing industries.

Newspaper circulation will not die, but it will fade, and large sections of the paper will go unread. Morning coffee will be shared by spouses not over the paper, but over the laptop. There isn't a need to put up with a product that offends, and Americans won't.

It used to be that the brand made the byline. Now the byline makes the brand. That's a key thing to keep in mind.

Until recently, when the *New York Times* announced the addition of a new columnist to its op-ed page, that meant a sort of instant influence had been bestowed on some writer. No more. Sure, these writers have some influence, just as the various fortresses along the Maginot Line had some influence on the early days of Germany's invasion of France.

Just not the sort of influence the French generals thought those fortresses would have.

Now that writers and reporters, pundits and everyone with a keyboard has access to publishing technology, there are no gates to keep, no power to say no to anyone. The "mainstream" was always an invention of elites, of course, but now it can no longer be defined by elites using a veto to block the appearance or transmission of ideas deemed unacceptable by elites.

This is invigorating but also potentially dangerous. Demagogues will, no doubt, try to use the blogosphere even as hate groups have, to identify and motivate their followers. Cults with terrible intent can do the same thing. Islamist fanatics have been using the web for years. The potential for evil to manipulate blogs is, of course, always present. Indeed, in a column I wrote for the **WeeklyStandard.com** last year, I speculated about the potential for "black blog operations," blogs that appear to be for a candidate or a cause only to turn on him, her, or it at a crucial moment. There is the potential for much mischief in any blog that has a large number of visitors. As noted, bad exit polling information infiltrated the blogosphere on November 2 and came close to having a dire effect.

But that potential for evil and mischief shouldn't stop anyone from exploring and using the new world of the blogosphere, any more than caution ought to have stopped people from looking into television or radio when they made their appearances. Fear or enthusiasm really doesn't matter. The blogosphere is a fact as real as a brick, and even though bricks can be used to build houses or hospitals or be thrown through windows or at heads, the reality of bricks doesn't change.

The changes sweeping through the news media are vast and tremendously disruptive of old hierarchies. But they are not limited to the news media. They are coming to your life and probably have already appeared there. That's what this book is: a giant flare directing your attention to the explosion of new media activity.

The key to keep in mind is that trust drives everything. To build and maintain trust is a tremendously difficult thing, requiring patient attention to detail and discipline over long periods of time. Mistakes by bloggers will be forgiven, but not deception and certainly not stubborn attachment to falsehood. As you explore the blogosphere and perhaps enter it or assign others to do so, put the "trust" question on the table and keep it there.

In a world changing as rapidly as ours is, only those who have earned and continue to earn trust will be in a position to influence the choices of third parties. Blogs can earn that most valuable commodity. Which is why you have to get started. Your competitors already have.

APPENDIX A

EARLY WRITINGS ON BLOGGING

I wrote my first internet column on the rise of new media on June 12, 2001, for the web-based **WorldNetDaily.com**. Since then, both at **WorldNetDaily** and the *Daily Standard*, the online edition of the *Weekly Standard* found at **WeeklyStandard.com**, and in two previous books, *In, But Not Of: A Guide to Christian Ambition and the Desire to Influence the World* (Thomas Nelson, 2003) and *If It's Not Close, They Can't Cheat: Crushing the Democrats in Every Election, and Why Your Life Depends on It* (Thomas Nelson, 2004), I have written extensively on new media, and specifically on the rise of the blogs. This appendix collects those early writings.

WorldNetDaily, June 12, 2001:
Elite media's slips are showing
© 2001 WorldNetDaily.com

The left-tilt of the elite media in this country is no longer much in doubt. Examples of Democratic-cheerleading in the pages of the big newspapers or on CNN and NBC carry all the spark of a "dog bites man" headline. Ho-hum.

We are used to it. We turn to the FOX News Network, and subscribe to the *Wall Street Journal*, the *Weekly Standard*, *National Review* and click on WorldNetDaily and RealClearPolitics. Still, some Democratic-boosterism is so outrageous, and some lefty-pumps so large that they deserve note. Here are three.

First, I am proud to coin a new term: The Miller-McCain Gap. To calculate the gap, one must total the number of network television minutes devoted to John McCain and the number of minutes devoted to Zell Miller. (Yes, you have to include CNN even though no one's watching anymore.) McCain, of course, is the "maverick" Republican Senator who causes much heartburn within his caucus and is rewarded with huge amounts of ink by the Beltway press corps. Zell Miller plays the same role within the Democratic caucus but remains nearly invisible. Why? Because the producers of shows like Matthews' "Whiffleball" and Russert's "Meet the Cuomo Aide" love stories underscoring troubles within the GOP and avoid stories about problems between and among the Democrats. Keep score in your mind. The Miller-McCain gap is huge and growing. It neatly expresses all that is wrong with the networks (and why, by the way, FOX News is killing all other cable networks).

Example No. 2 of egregious media bias comes from, where else, the *Left Angeles Times*, a former newspaper now reconfigured as the press room for Gray Davis. In fact, Monday's paper carried an offering from Sacramento columnist "Slumberin'" George Skelton that set a new standard for obsequiousness to Davis, even by this "paper's" standards. It literally begins this way: "The phone rang and it was the governor. 'Just wanted to talk a little bit about electricity,' he said. 'I think we are on the verge of breaking the exorbitant spot market. . . .'" What follows is a full column that reads like the press release from the Davis re-election campaign, which is what it is. Not a whisper of a hard question from George; not one quote to the contrary from a GOP elected official to balance the governor's propaganda; and certainly not one line about the $30,000 a month in taxpayer dollars that Davis is pumping to Gore operatives turned "consultants," Mark Fabiani and Chris Lehane or their ongoing ties to Southern California Edison. Of course not, that would constitute reporting, and as such, is banned at the *Times*. Again, if you want to call this to the attention of the folks at the *Times*' mother ship, Chicago's Tribune Company, e-mail the chairman and the president of the newspaper division, John Madigan and Jack Fuller, respectively.

Example 3 is an indictment of the entire press corps, national and statewide in California. Last Thursday, the education bureaucrats at the California Department of Education issued a press release detailing the results of the first-ever administration of the California High School Exit Exam. The test was not given to seniors. In fact, no one has to pass the test until 2004. But the law says that beginning that year either you pass or no diploma. So it was given to freshmen to get an idea of the size of the problem. The results are stunning. But they were also camouflaged and the deception has apparently worked.

First, the Democrat in charge of the department lowered the "passing" score from the traditional 70 percent to 60 percent on the English section and 55 percent on the math. A few short stories on this ludicrous redefinition of "passing" followed (though I could not find one in the *Left Angeles Times*). These brief stories did not ask the obvious question: Using 70 percent, how many of the freshmen would have passed? Reporters also missed other obvious questions: "Why didn't you give seniors the test to establish a baseline from which improvement could be charted? Why didn't you give the test to students graduating from, say, Texas high schools to establish comparison data? Why didn't you publish the geographic break-down of test results?"

The reporting that did occur was stunning enough. Only 65 percent "passed" the English portion of the test, and only 45 percent "passed" the math portion (which means, of course, that less than 45 percent of these kids could earn a diploma today). Defenders of the California education establishment have written to me in the aftermath of a radio show on which I discussed these results to urge that these are freshmen and have three years of learning ahead of them. They are right of course, but no one is telling me what the expected level of improvement is. I am not an optimist.

I am not an optimist because the Department's calculated obfuscation about the depth of the problem is very revealing about the agenda of the education bureaucracy. Rather than set out the dismal facts and probe for the real level of learning, the Department is covering up from the get-go, lowering the "passing" bar and prettying up the prospects. Absent a hard look at the real data, who can trust these people or the unGovernor to tell us the truth. Sure, the kids will get plenty of chances to pass the test, but my guess is that the test will be jettisoned or so dumbed-down as to mean nothing. And another generation of students will be sacrificed in the service of political careers.

So there you have three examples of naked media bias: Over-reporting McCain; glowing coverage of Gray Davis; and non-coverage of the public school meltdown in California. As I wrote above, it's just more "Dog Bites Man."

WorldNetDaily, July 10, 2001:
New Media: Sticking it to the old boys
© 2001 WorldNetDaily.com

Today, July 10, marks the first anniversary of my radio program.

I set two goals a year ago: To be syndicated to 20 markets and to have achieved a significant share in the hyper-competitive 6 to 9 a.m. Los Angeles market. The show is now heard in more than 40 markets, including coveted morning drive slots in Denver, Minneapolis-St. Paul, Phoenix, San Diego, Seattle and Tucson and communities as diverse as Boston and Louisville, Honolulu and Tampa Bay. Starting with an almost zero existing audience in Los Angeles, the program is now the second-highest rated talk show there in the morning, and the ratings have far outpaced even the most optimistic projections.

Success is never random, but as the old saying goes, it has many fathers, while failure is an orphan. If I am correct about the primary reason behind the growth, however, there are implications beyond the offices of program directors and general managers in radio stations across the U.S.

It's a given that media success requires communication ability, and I have got that. Guests matter as well, and my regular contributors—Fred Barnes and Morton Kondracke, Virginia Postrel and Kellyanne Fitzpatrick Conway, Terry Eastland, Erwin Chemerinsky and John Eastman to name just a few—guarantee the listeners sharp and informed insights into national politics. Folks do care about what the government's up to, so a weekly visit from the Chair of the House Rules Committee David Dreier provides that, as have the parade of electeds from the GOP. A sprinkling of lefties like my old friend Bill Press adds salt. I have added regular features on news from the spheres of religion, literature and, of course, the movies, in order to report on all facets of American life. And our addiction to the often-horrific music of the late '60s and early '70s does draw in the crucial radio demographic of adults aged 25 to 54. (Those who have never heard the show will not understand producer Duane's and engineer Adam's unique roles in this regard.)

The product, then, is very good. But many good products do not succeed. Why has this one? Two crucial reasons.

First, the collapse of credibility in American media has left the field open to those who will honestly announce their points of view and fairly present their perspectives. The sophistication of the American consumer when it comes to the news media is not to be underestimated. There is a reason why the big three net-works have lost their collective grip on the news business, and it didn't start with calling Florida for Gore, though that may have put a period at the end of the long, rambling sentence that a Rather broadcast has become. There is a reason why American newspapers are widely ridiculed. And there is a reason behind the rise of the FOX News Network.

More than half of America does not trust the news media. They believe it—accurately—to be filled to the brim with agenda journalists who will not only shade the truth, but who will also almost inevitably distort it, ignore it when inconvenient, and sometimes outright trample upon it for the purpose of advancing the causes of the left. On issue after issue, including the most obvious ones of reproductive rights, environmental protection, defense preparedness, and campaign finance, the agenda of elite opinion-makers is fixed firmly in the camp of the left side of the left-leaning Democratic Party. This is a given, and not even much debated anymore. But the effect of this decline by media elites into boosterism for liberals is the triumph—now unfolding—of the market in matters related to news consumption.

Credit must be given where huge credit is due. Rush Limbaugh was the pioneer, the broadcast journalism equivalent of Lewis and Clark. His double proposition—that politics mattered deeply to huge numbers of people and that the center-right was unrepresented on the airwaves—has been proven beyond doubt in the only measure that matters in the media marketplace, audience size. Limbaugh is the most influential journalist in America, period.

Roger Ailes was watching, and this entrepreneur of ideas provisioned a wagon train to the center-right called the FOX News Network and the ratings success in the world of cable could not have been more dramatic. CNN had anchored itself on the left side, and went from the Clinton News Network to the Collapsing News Network. CNBC and MSNBC somehow convinced themselves that Chris Matthews and Tim Russert (a former Tip O'Neil and former Mario Cuomo aide respectively) could earn the trust of center-right America, and threw in Jonathan Alter to keep the way-left happy. Ailes must scratch his head some nights, wondering how long the television gods will favor him with mule-headed ideologues at the competition's helm.

My program's launch and take-off have been powered by the same dynamic. Rush works different hours from me, and Hume, O'Reilly, and Hannity work nights. When I attend to the center-right, nobody else in America is doing so. A monopoly on an approach in a time-slot is a very good thing to have.

Now to the second key. I am a skilled editor because God has blessed me with a pretty rare quality: news judgment.

There are vast numbers of Americans who care passionately about the news and their country. But they are pressed for time, and awash in a sea of choices. Most newspapers are hopelessly late in a news cycle that never ends, and many of them (think the *Left*

Angeles Times) are just laughable on matters of importance to the center-right.

(An aside: The *Times* ran a full page ad this week trumpeting the paper's three new opinion columnists, Peter King, John Balzar and Steve Lopez—the Huey, Dewey, and Louie of the left. This trio joins Sacramento-based Slumberin' George Skelton to guarantee *Times'* readers 14 versions of the same thing each and every week, proving conclusively not only everything I have written above, but also this paper's collapse into a House of Mirrors for a frightened and aging crowd of '60s crusaders, who collectively seem to believe if you talk to yourself long enough, that must mean nobody else matters.)

So what are these information-hungry news consumers doing? They are selecting new editors. It's as simple as that. My ratings are surging because I am both a pretty good commentator and a pretty good editor.

Virtually unnoticed by the viziers of the opinion elite, an unstoppable threat to their information hegemony has arisen on the radio and now on the web. Others have found a way of communicating with the public about the priority that stories and perspectives ought to be given. The Left has mistaken Rush as a commentator. He is that, of course, but he is also an editor. So is Brit Hume. So is Tony Snow on Sunday morning. And since July 10 of last year, so am I. And America wants new editors, to quote the vice president, "big time."

On my list of favorite websites, there are two that represent what I am talking about. *Reason* magazine editor-at-large Virginia Postrel runs Vpostrel.com. Intellectual-at-large and utility infielder of the center-left Mickey Kaus runs Kausfiles.com. Postrel and Kaus have become—for me and for other visitors to their sites—editors of a huge, indeed unquantifiable torrent of news and information, all of which has been made available to every computer owner via the Web. So, for that matter, have Drudge and Andrew Sullivan, the "best of the web" feature of the *Wall Street Journal*'s Opinion Journal and Lucianne.com. There are scores of others. Traffic cops with commentary added in, you might easily mistake these sites as indulgent "me-zines" but they are really just the first wave of UbeR-editors to claim this role. Yes, they give their own two cents' worth, but they are primarily interested in sending you to the "good stuff."

Another category of websites, including of course WorldNetDaily, as well as RealClearPolitics.com and Free Republic are staffed by more than a single pair of hands, but these sites too are quickly establishing themselves as alternatives to news room and network hierarchies when it comes to directing America's collective attention to this or that story.

Eventually, a new elite of web and radio editors will emerge, and their collective impact will be as great as that of the big bosses at the *New York Times*, the *Washington Post* and the *Wall Street Journal*. They will begin to set the news cycle, to cue the horde of worker bees in the world of journalism, to drive the stories. And they will do so because the staffs of the newsgathering organizations will have to listen or be left behind.

My show has enjoyed a wonderful inaugural year because I have earned the trust of my audience not only as a commentator, but also as an editor. That elusive gift—news judgment—is the key to all media. Are you reporting or commenting on the stories/ controversies/ issues/ events/ hobbies about which large numbers of Americans have an interest? Do they trust you to anticipate in their curiosity? And do they trust you to lay it out fairly, and to announce your opinions as just that, opinions, and not facts?

The old elites have substituted their political enthusiasms in the place of news judgment, and they gave up on fairness long ago. My audience trusts me to pick the stories that matter, and to present them with my commentary and with various viewpoints —and humor—mixed in. It seems to be working.

WorldNetDaily, October 2, 2001:
Contemptible commentators
© 2001 WorldNetDaily.com

Revolutions swept Europe in 1848, and when order returned a year later, many of the leaders of the revolutionaries were con- demned to die. The ruler of Austria at the time was a regent, Prince Felix Schwarzenberg. His advisers approached him and urged mercy for the rebel generals.

"Mercy by all means," Schwarzenberg replied, "mercy is a very good thing. But first let us have a little hanging."

No reasonable person proposes the hanging of—or any vio- lence whatsoever against—those who chose the hour of America's tragedy to snarl at her greatness, her military, or her president. But in the place of a little hanging, let us insist on a great deal of clarity. In the aftermath of the tidal wave of terror and murder that struck the U.S. on September 11, there is a giant undertow of common sense and clarity. It has sucked a number of posers out to sea. I do not think we should ignore or forget their moral cowardice or their petty vanity. Others directly con- trol the employment fate of the scores of offending parties. The commentariat can do nothing except mark clearly the distasteful remarks rendered by many and their disingenuous defenses that followed the public outcry against them.

Peter Jennings sniffed his way through the day of the attack, remarking that some presidents are better than others at rallying the country. He is said to be hurt that millions of viewers thought him objectionable. He was.

Maureen Dowd of the *New York Times*, on the day after the attack, thought it was necessary to attack the president's move- ments on September 11, sneering that "even the president did not know where to go." That the president had just ordered the shoot-down of his fellow citizens, or the enormity of the fact that timed attacks on the nation's landmarks had occurred did not cause her to hesitate then or apologize since. She used her column on the last day of September to continue her counter-attack on her critics. Citing her immigrant father and his military and police service, Ms. Dowd wrote that "I don't need instructions from Ari Fleisher, the White House press secretary, on the conduct of a good American." Perhaps not instructions, just practice. Ms. Dowd used the balance of her column to attack the Bush team as "image profiteers" dishing out "hyperventilated spin," and to claim that "[w]e should dread a climate where the jobs of columnists and comedians are endangered by dissent."

I get it. We should be thanking her for her attacks on the president and her lame defenses of those attacks. Our way of life depends on Maureen Dowd's column. Why hadn't I seen it before?

Bill Maher, already well known for comparing the retarded to dogs and the faithful to fools, is in the same ditch with Dowd. He struck his blow for freedom on the first broadcast after the attack: "We have been the cowards," proclaimed Maher, "lobbing cruise missiles from 2,000 miles away. That's cowardly. Staying in the airplane when it hits the building, say what you want about it, it's not cowardly."

Jerry Falwell and Pat Robertson assured that the right did not go unrepresented in the parade of offensive remarks—though Falwell alone, among the names listed here, has had the grace to abjectly apologize. Andy Rooney, well into his dotage, tried to argue that President Bush did not know that Afghanistan was landlocked when the president made frequent reference to countries "harboring" terrorists. He has clung to his argument, aware, perhaps that the truth that he thought it funny to mock the president's intelligence at a moment of national peril was more dangerous than being thought merely stupid and stubborn.

There are other candidates for the pundits' hall of shame, but now we have the inevitable attempt to rally around the offenders, claiming that the First Amendment is at stake. Dowd did not invent this tactic. *The Los Angeles* Times television "critic" Howard Rosenberg, who waited until Friday after the attack to conclude that the president "has seemed almost like a little boy at times—a kid with freckles wishing he were somewhere else," found no one to defend him so he defended himself this past week. Sure enough, he grabbed for the First Amendment, demonstrating either ignorance of the Amendment's concern with government censorship and not public revulsion or the abject desperation of a horse's rump finally found out. He is now, and will forever remain, the Ted Baxter of his trade.

Rosenberg tried to save face by admitting his timing "stunk," but declaring boldly he has no regrets. Then in a stunning display of cliché for a television "critic," he argued that his detractors—they were legion and the *Times* is begging the subscribers via letters not to blame Howard on the whole paper—were "America right or wrong types." "If this myopic dictum is followed, the U.S. media might as well pack away their megaphones and allow their 1st Amendment liberties to atrophy. If it had been followed by journalists reporting about Vietnam, My Lai and other excesses from that debacle would still be interred along with the bones of victims."

And there you have it. Maher and Jennings, Dowd and Rosenberg—all the fools caught in the undertow are laying claim to hero status. It hasn't worked and it won't. Maher seems doomed though Disney's boss Michael Eisner has yet to OK his cancellation despite sponsor revulsion and audience disgust. Eisner runs Jennings as well, and that aging icon will never get bumped, but a great deal of audience has fled. Rosenberg would never get the boot from *Times* management, though the Chicago suits at the Tribune Company have to wonder about the paper's declining circulation and its steady march into irrelevance. Rooney wouldn't be there another week if Don Hewitt was alive. Falwell and Robertson work for God, and Dowd works for Howell Raines, who thinks he's God, so those three will find their rebukes in the privacy of quiet chats. Others have been fired. Tenure protects the rest. But it doesn't matter who stays and who goes.

What matters, and what is simply irreversible, is the crashing even further down of any idea that elites in this country have any idea about what the country is really all about. Every one of these named and scores of others simply do not understand the country that protects their foolishness. All of them have skills. Not one has wisdom about the country, and most lack even basic knowledge.

They will resist this self-knowledge, though all around them will whisper about it for years to come: In the test of their careers, they flunked. The journalists are particularly cursed. Such tests come only once in a lifetime. They join the November 1941 critics of FDR, and the critics of Churchill throughout the late '30s and the Reagan bashers after Reykjavik. We don't remember the names of any of these, except as I just have, with a generalized and deep contempt.

We do not need a little hanging. It is already done.

In the midst of a heated political battle, I was alone in pushing for a particular strategy. I stubbornly held my ground. One of my colleagues quoted her mother-in-law, a native of Ireland: "When everyone says you're drunk, you'd better sit down."

Ms. Dowd, Mr. Rosenberg, Mr. Rooney and the rest: You'd better sit down.

WorldNetDaily, December 11, 2001:
Irrelevant cleverness
© 2001 WorldNetDaily.com

Three months ago, terrorists launched a devastating attack on America that claimed several thousand dead and thousands more wounded, and shocked and shook the entire nation. The president rallied the country and ordered the execution of the military's plan for reprisal. The plan's first stage is largely and successfully complete. There are enormous concerns, of course, and a long and dangerous struggle is still ahead. But more has been learned—relearned, actually—about this country and its people in the past three months than in the past 30 years.

So, as the 90-day anniversary of the attacks approaches, upon what are the elites of the left focused?

Run through the Sunday papers from Dec. 9: In the *Washington Post*, Michael Kinsley has filed an attack on Ari Fleisher for being boring and evasive. In the *New York Times*, Maureen Dowd is essaying on the translation of Harry Potter into Latin. The "featured writer" of the *Los Angeles Times* is John Balzar, and the paper has invested much in the effort to make him a "must read" on both coasts. There's a reason you haven't heard of him—he uses his column this Sunday past to extol his credentials as a "connoisseur of microbrew beer" as he defends alcohol and its users. Over at the *Boston Globe*, Ellen Goodman at least works the word "Afghanistan" into her big piece for the week. But the column is an attack on our military's dress code for women deployed in Saudi Arabia.

Two days after the 60th anniversary of Pearl Harbor and on the eve of a national look back at a fall of savagery, fear, regrouping and bravery unlike any other in our history, and a quartet of representatives from the political and cultural left all chose to write on small matters irrelevant to the drama before us and before the world. Not only did they make these choices, their editors gave them the space to do so. I wonder what Walter Lippmann chose to write on in early March of 1942?

Whether they have nothing to say or are still stunned by their sudden and nearly complete irrelevance, this simultaneous reach for absurd subjects underscores some obvious but hard truths about the pen-pushers on America's left.

All of these people are clever writers. Once again, cleverness is revealed as unrelated to wisdom. Wars always reveal this. And it is always forgotten in a long peace. The locust years of the last presidency elevated the clever people higher than they had ever got before, because there was no substance there at all, just words. Now they are stumbling around. These folks have tried to write about the serious things, but have hit the wrong note every time. Poor Ms. Dowd may have set a record for outrageous misses. No wonder she is regressing to her high school days and writing of the difficulty she had translating Caesar's "Commentaries."

We also have to relearn that pretensions to seriousness are not the same thing as seriousness. Kinsley may never be the same since being knocked around by O'Reilly, but truth be told he's never been significant in the way that George Will or Charles Krauthammer has been. Balzar won't get out of AA ball, and if Goodman has penned a memorable column in her life, I missed it.

These and many others have risen because they share attitudes (they don't deserve the higher tag of "ideas") with the hiring editors and the column buyers. Attitude was enough during the long stretch of years after the fall of the Soviet empire when folks demanded peace dividends and argued with straight faces that HMO reform should take precedence over national defense and foreign affairs. All of a sudden, we need serious analysis from serious people and it turns out the wittiest people from the college papers are running the show. What a surprise: They have nothing to say.

It is common now to note how little time was spent on terrorism in the three presidential and one vice presidential debates last fall. Don't blame President Bush or Vice President Gore—they weren't asking the questions. And you really can't blame just Jim Lehrer. He was the perfect distillation of center-left attitude in the country, and a gentleman to boot. Go back and watch the tapes of Russert during the campaign. After Vice President Cheney's selection was announced, he made the obligatory appearance on Meet the Cuomo Aide. The first seven questions dealt with his heart condition. Not much talk of that now.

Try finding a single elite media commentator who spoke or wrote seriously about the dangers in the world and the first priorities in presidential selection during the fall of 2000. There was at least one—I thought at the time that this writer made a crucial point on the Thursday before the presidential election. In fact, rereading the last four paragraphs of Peggy Noonan's *Wall Street Journal* column of November 2, 2000, I am convinced that Noonan deserves the Nostradamus Award as well as a Pulitzer. Here is what she wrote 13 months ago:

> Mr. Bush is at odds with the spirit of the past 8 years in another way. He appears to be wholly uninterested in lying, has no gift for it, thinks it's wrong.
>
> This is important at any time, but is crucial now. The next president may well be forced to shepherd us through the first nuclear event since World War II, the first terrorist attack or missile attack. "Man has never had a weapon he didn't use,"

Ronald Reagan said in conversation, and we have been most fortunate man has not used these weapons to kill in the past 50 years. But half the foreign and defense policy establishment fears, legitimately, that the Big Terrible Thing is coming, whether in India-Pakistan, or in Asia or in lower Manhattan.

When it comes, if it comes, the credibility—the trust-worthiness—of the American president will be the key to our national survival. We may not be able to sustain a president who is known for his tendency to tell untruths.

If we must go through a terrible time, a modest man of good faith is the one we'll need in charge. That is George Herbert Walker Bush, governor of Texas.

Yes, she really did write that more than a year ago, and it has far more relevance and power than any or all of the four offerings mentioned above which appeared on December 9, 2001. The point is, as the coach said to the sprinter who asked to be made fast in *Chariots of Fire*, "You can't put in what God left out."

God left seriousness, wisdom, and perspective out of most writers, as well as political judgment. A few, like Ms. Noonan, got all the gifts. We ought to read the latter, and ask the former to find a better outlet for their cleverness. We haven't the time to spare anymore.

WorldNetDaily, August 14, 2002:
The growing power of the blog
© 2002 WorldNetDaily.com

I am not now, nor have I ever been, a blogaholic. Sure, I visit a few blogs every day, and I check **Instapundit** every few hours. I have been known to vanish into The Corner at National Review for long stretches, and I can't understand why Virginia Postrel can't spare even 10 minutes a day from her new manuscript to update the Dynamist. But I am not hooked. I can stop whenever I want.

I read **Mickey Kaus** and **Andrew Sullivan** when they were both just ink-stained wretches, and I interviewed **Eugene Volokh** when he was wearing academic short-pants. Now that they have been absorbed into the Borg, er, Blog, they are just more available, not particularly different. But their collective power is growing. Growing rapidly, in fact.

Something very big is happening here, as was the case when radio gave print a big elbow, and then when television gave radio a huge body blow. The fourth generation has arrived, and it is wild out there. If you are a writer and not yet hit by the web-scrum, wait until your work attracts the cybermob. You will never again be that lazy when it comes to fact-checking. This is the most obvious and most noted of the effects of the rise of the Blog.

Before long, however, the greybeards in the world of web-player-wannabes are going to figure out that the blogocracy matters a great deal in generating traffic to their sites, and the scramble to link to the big blogs will be on. I hope Glenn Reynolds, the force behind **Instapundit.com**, turns aside offers from all but either the *Washington Post* or the *New York Times*. If a center-right blog marries a center-left paper, the offspring would be good for American politics and journalism.

Other changes have to be in the offing. The success of **The Corner**, wherein *National Review*'s online editors and contributors talk to each other in full public view, heralds similar spaces at all major sites (can WorldNetDaily be far behind, or the *Washington Times* and *Weekly Standard*?).

The key link will emerge between radio and blogdom. Even as print and television have increasingly found themselves allied on the cable networks, the decentralization of both radio and the bloggers allows them to serve each other in a very healthy symbiosis. As a host, I need guests with brains and sharp opinions. Bloggers covet traffic which a network radio show can provide. The bloggers, in turn, send their readers to *my site* and the circle is complete.

The most revolutionary effect of blogging is still a ways off. The first three generations of media are remarkably age-, race- and gender-driven. What had originally been a reserve of white males is now a region of tortuous balancing and hypersensitive massaging of unspoken quotas. The blogosphere has none of that. It is the real marketplace of ideas, where there is no barrier to entry and Ragged Dick doesn't have to sell papers for very long if he's got talent.

As a result, there will be no forced retirement from the web if the blogger is deemed "too old" to keep a viewer's eye. In fact, looks and voice matter not at all. And neither do the political tastes of the editor-in-chief or the loony lefty on the city desk. Traffic is traffic and it can be measured and the market is the judge. If you can blog with effect until you are 95, more power to you.

And if you are 16, but brilliant, write this way, please.

Ultimately, the blogs force a choice upon you: If you join in and have the goods, you are opting out of elected life and any prayer of eventual judicial or other high-level governmental selection because candor is the first requirement of successful blogging . . . and there is no erasing your past work.

But if you can set aside those ambitions, the world of blogging is where the life of the mind has moved. Genuine argument is emerging from the stranglehold that the bigs of the first three generations have imposed upon it. "Cut and thrust" is back, and a web duel makes light sabers look tame. As a center-right conservative confident of the ideas on my side, this means very good things indeed.

Cheers to the revolution.

The *Daily Standard*, January 15, 2003
The Other Bias

There's another insidious form of media discrimination: Against astute political observers on the West Coast. by Hugh Hewitt 01/15/2003 12:00:00 AM

EUGENE VOLOKH AND JOHN EASTMAN are not household names. Both teach constitutional law, Volokh at UCLA and Eastman at Chapman University. Both arrived in the classroom after clerking for big names in the courts—Volokh for Ninth Circuit Judge Alex Kozinski and Supreme Court Justice Sandra Day O'Connor, and Eastman for Fourth Circuit Judge J. Michael Luttig and Justice Clarence Thomas. And both are prolific writers on subjects legal and political. Volokh helps run one of the most referenced blogs in the country, the **Volokh Conspiracy**, and Eastman's writing usually appears at the website of the **Claremont Institute**.

The two professors also bring to their work the experiences of careers that preceded legal training. Eastman has a Ph.D. from the Claremont Graduate School and served in the Reagan administration as spokesman for the Civil Rights Commission before even beginning law school. Volokh, who emigrated from the Soviet Union in 1975 at the age of 7, spent six years as a computer programmer after finishing his undergraduate studies at UCLA in 1983. (That's right, he was 15 when he finished college with a B.S. in Math-Computer Science.)

Both men are anti-eggheads, spirited but courteous debaters with ready laughs and winsome appeal. Both have often appeared on my radio program and always inspire a tide of e-mails asking for more time with them. Professor Eastman is usually matched against one of the best the left has to offer on constitutional matters, Erwin Chemerinsky from the USC law school, and that pair manages to make interesting even the farther reaches of the high court's docket. Volokh has specialties in unusual areas, including Second Amendment rights.

They are, in short, perfect pundits—knowledgeable and compelling, informed and opinionated.

So why don't you see them on "Hardball," "Donahue," "O'Reilly," "Hannity & Colmes," "This Week," "The News Hour," etc.? Is Howard Fineman that good? Is the American viewing public demanding more and more of pollster Mark Penn? Eastman estimates he makes about three national broadcast appearances a year; Volokh puts the number at five. Thus, two of the brightest public intellectuals in America combine to opine before a national audience eight times a year. My guess is that their output totals about 30 television minutes. Why so low?

The answer has nothing to do with a left-right bias, or a Republican-Democrat tilt. It is simple geography: These are two of the best that the West Coast has to offer, but the Washington–New York bookers are generally unfamiliar with the rising stars of political debate, and they are especially so when those stars are working in Pacific Standard Time.

In the past year some new faces are beginning to punch through the lineups of aging, and usually predictable guests in opinion land. Peter Beinart from the New Republic and the *Washington Monthly*'s **Joshua Micah Marshall** have begun to be seen as solid .300 hitters. But the hunt for new faces usually ends at the borders of New York and D.C. There are two reasons for this.

It often costs money to use out-of-studio guests, and not just the cost of the car, but the studio time if there is no network facility nearby.

And hosts lose valuable eye-to-eye contact with a guest a continent away, which diminishes production values.

But those costs do not approach the loss of excluding the Volokhs and the Eastmans from the nightly dust-ups, not to mention the scores of other opinion-purveyors in fly-over land. The cable shows especially are struggling for audience, and only the FOX News Channel is making any progress. Maybe viewers outside of the Beltway are not interested in all-Beltway-all-the-time. Maybe if the net were cast a bit wider, a greater audience would follow a greater variety of guests.

Beyond ratings self-interest is the even more pressing issue of the responsibility of television news executives to work diligently at getting the entire story onto the airwaves. The D.C. opinion corps inevitably suffers from the same information gaps of any headquarters far removed from its front lines, no matter whether the business is sales or war. It shows and the audience knows.

The *Daily Standard*, June 4, 2003
The Big Four
How a small quartet of blogs is poised to remake the political landscape as the '04 election cycle begins.

JOSHUA MICAH MARSHALL is frustrated. He's the young-Blumenthal-in-training of partisan punditry, but in recent days his favorite story line can't get any traction. "It's amazing what it takes to start a feeding frenzy these days," he lamented at **Talking Points Memo,** his web log, last week.

Marshall has been flogging his Tom-Delay-is-Magneto story for what seems to be a year, and it has been largely ignored not just by elite newspapers, but also by the blogosphere. An opinion storm requires certain ingredients to conjure it, and in the world of the blogosphere in 2003, you need one of the Big Four to buy in.

The Big Four are **Instapundit, Andrew Sullivan, Mickey Kaus,** and **The Volokh Conspiracy.** These four sites are usually visited by news junkies many times a day because they are staffed by bright people and continually updated, and thus they can guide the chattering class to a breaking story or even a hitherto ignored story. Trent Lott is no longer majority leader in part because these superpowers of the blog filed and fueled the story of his remarks at Strom's birthday bash. The *New York Times* is reeling because of consistent attention to its inaccuracies and biases by these same sites. Because these sites are so widely read and referred to, they can amplify even small murmurs and overnight can redirect traditional media towards a target.

The power of synchronized blogging is still somewhat incipient. The first generation of bloggers are individualists, and unlikely to coordinate their activities. But if blog alliances do begin to develop among them, the ability to drive the news cycle in a particular direction will be immense.

When the blogosphere ignores a story, that story is marked as boring or insignificant or both. If a story cannot hold the interest of the web's news hounds, it is hardly likely to interest the general reading or viewing public.

If the web seizes on a story, however, it is a huge signal to editors and assignment desks to pay attention. The media dinosaurs can ignore these currents in opinion-making, of course, but not for long.

The first presidential election with full blog participation is opening now. As the Iowa caucuses approach, watch the blogs (1) to see if any Democrat is catching fire there and (2) for leaks of damaging info. Howard Dean is reported to be investing heavily in controlling web-spin, but the blogs cannot be controlled in any meaningful way. The filters that reporters and producers used to provide are gone, destroyed by free agents in cyberspace. **The Drudge Report**, a sort of Model-T blog, did much to bedevil Clinton. If any of the Big Four reach Drudge-status, it will be as though King Kong, Godzilla, and Mothra all arrived in an Iowa China shop at the same time.

Theodore White began his account of the 1964 presidential campaign this way: "Every man who writes of politics shapes unknowingly in his mind some fanciful metaphor to embrace all the wild, apparently erratic events and personalities in the process he tries to describe."

It is crazy to try and develop a metaphor for the new politics—a politics of a 24/7 news cycle, cable land, talk radio, **Free Republic.com**, and **DemocraticUnderground.com**, and thousands of blogs—but the opening scene from "Gangs of New York" comes to mind. Campaigns would be well-advised to designate a team just to keep track of and respond to web-generated stories and opinion, starting with the Big Four.

The *Daily Standard*, July 17, 2003
Memo To: Editors and Editorial Page Editors
From: Readers
Subject: Lileks

IT HAS COME TO OUR ATTENTION that your editorial pages
are predictable, repetitive, and usually cranky. The worst among
you think it is somehow daring and perhaps even courageous to
run the fevers of Robert Scheer. The timid recoil at the thought of
providing both Will and Krauthammer on a weekly basis for fear
of turning the readers into members of the "undead Halliburton
Zombie Army," as Lileks puts it.

That's Lileks, as in James Lileks, columnist for Newhouse
News Service and the *Minneapolis Star Tribune*, and quite possibly the funniest guy you have never heard of.

At least we hope you've never heard of him, or his blog, The
Bleat, because otherwise you have no excuse for having denied
him to your readers while peddling Ellen Goodman or some other
old-as-the-planets and dull as dirt culture-war left-over. Lileks is
quite obviously the best generally unknown columnist in America,
and among the top two in North America when you add in
Canadian Mark Steyn. (I won't choose between these two because
both are featured weekly guests on my radio show, and if either
gets really upset with me, I could end up a featured item in one of
their columns, which is not good for one's reputation.—HH)

It is hard to be funny. Genuinely funny writers can be listed
quickly: Dave Barry, P.J. O'Rourke, Christopher Buckley. We'll
include Joseph Epstein and Calvin Trilling on our list—though
their humor is of a very elevated sort—and Chris Erskine, Matt
Labash, and Larry Miller deserve a spot on the "certain to make
you smile" log.

Steyn and Lileks are laugh-out-loud writers and pundits with punch. Lileks, incredibly, delivers five mirth-inducing reads for free each week on his website. His Sunday column for the *Strib* is a homey, chatty, and unfailingly amusing look at the ordinary absurdity of life—a welcome break from the sermons and raised eyebrows of the opinion sections and book reviews. It is written for an audience of Minnesocoldians, but it absorbs the attention of even jaded California denizens. Like his Newhouse columns, Lileks's *Strib* work could run in every paper in America.

Why then doesn't it? On an objective basis, Lileks is wildly popular among readers who get a chance to read him. The same with Steyn. You can test our assertion by a visit to **technorati.com**, which allows you to check the blogosphere's connectivity ratings. Lileks is widely linked to and commented upon, and his fans stretch across the vast political spectrum of the internet's chattering class. This is a sure sign of broad appeal because the weak are never recognized by the blogosphere and the old and the lazy are mercilessly culled from the herd. Lileks is prospering on the web because Lileks is good.

I GET NO SHARE in Lileks's profits and have no interest in his rise to international stardom except the almost certainly vain hope that he will help me through four days of broadcasting from the Minnesota State Fair. I write about his relative obscurity because it illustrates a point that needs to be made again and again: Newspapers and TV talking heads are falling behind their audiences because they refuse to read the map that is in front of their noses. They want to regain their monopoly on commentary, and seem to believe that by ignoring the repeated tidal waves that hit them, they can will themselves back to relevance.

The wise editor would instead allow the battle of the blogs to throw up champions and then ink them to multiyear commentary deals. MSNBC figured this out with Glenn Reynolds, but the ink-and-paper crowd is still busy debating whether they ought to dignify talk radio with coverage (even though that audience dwarfs their own). Horse-and-buggy editors can't even dream of learning how to navigate the cyber-pundits beyond Romenesko, the media critic at Poynter.org.

Newspaper readers like me want newspapers to survive for at least a few more decades. To do that, the dinosaurs have to get out of the swamp. That means finding and printing the best writers and employing the best reporters. For the former, at least, that means Lileks.

The *Daily Standard*, June 17, 2004
Black Blog Ops
Blogs are popular and influential, but could they be used for political dirty tricks? Or worse?

WHEN WILL George Smiley and Karla begin to blog?

Smiley and Karla are the two central characters from John Le Carre's finest set of Cold War intelligence thrillers. Smiley was the best of the operatives, patiently wending his way through misinformation and misdirection, deceptions and deceits.

In the era of Reagan, everything had to be understood as admitting of at least two interpretations. Was your information genuine or planted, or did the Soviets or East Germans or someone else want you to think it was planted, and would you let them know that you knew? It was wonderful stuff—moles, tradecraft, honeypots, and Cubans attached to the United Nations.

Fifteen years after the fall of the Berlin Wall, we are a much less suspicious people when it comes to disinformation. Which brings us to the blogosphere.

Time magazine discovered blogs this week, with an extensive article on their proliferation and impact. "Not that long ago, blogs were one of those annoying buzz words that you could safely get away with ignoring," the authors admit. But not anymore. They go on to declare that "Bloggers are inverting the cozy media hierarchies of yore."

True enough. Like a reverse Atlantis, a new archipelago of opinion and news providers has risen up from nowhere to drive stories and news cycles. So we should be asking about the potential for deception in the format. The web is widely used and relied upon. It would not be hard for intelligence services from around the world to build blogs with an intent to deceive or manipulate, putting out solid content to gain an initial audience before using it to disseminate disinformation intentionally.

Similarly, the inevitable backstab blog has to be on some political consultant's mind. Get it started and growing as a pro candidate X blog. Build an audience via tried and true techniques—including the purchase of blog-ads—and then, late in a campaign, have the blog turn on candidate X. If any of the high profile lefties at work today—the DailyKos or Atrios, for example—were to suddenly turn on Kerry, citing implausibility fatigue, for example—that would be news and a blow to Kerry. Could Kos really be working for Rove? The costs of starting a blog are so low that the mischief potential is quite high.

ALSO, a portion of the war on terror is being fought over the internet, with radical Islamist groups routinely employing websites to project their messages and their demands. How long before our intelligence services or those of our allies begin to turn that technology back upon the terrorists? Or might the People's Republic of China—always in the vanguard of espionage—figure out that pro-PRC blogs might be a good thing to subsidize for the long haul, perhaps without owning up to the sponsorship?

In recent months, the Belmont Club has exploded onto the blogging scene, powered by impressive analysis of the war and its stakes. In less than six months, more than 1,100,000 visitors have stopped by to sample "Wretchard's" writings. I have had an e-mail exchange with Wretchard, and believe him to be what he says he is—just an amateur analyst making his views known. But his success got me to thinking about the potential for the use of blogs to shape opinions by dressing partisans up as new and anonymous sources. Which then got me to thinking about governments using the new medium to play public opinion. Which led to the idea of hostile movements doing the same.

Calling James Jesus Angleton. It is a brave new blogging world, and mischief beyond the easily spotted inanities of the MoveOn.org crowd will no doubt follow.

Chapter 32 from *In, But Not Of: A Guide to Christian Ambition and the Desire to Influence the World* (Nashville, TN: Thomas Nelson, 2003).

START AND MAINTAIN A WEB LOG (BLOG)

You may already know what a blog is—an online diary of your thoughts on whatever crosses your mind. The dominant blog of the day—judging by number of visitors daily—is Instapundit.com by Tennessee law professor Glenn Reynolds. There are literally thousands more. They represent the most important communications development of the new century. Join the revolution. Start a blog.

You need a web address and some idea of how to post. This will be second nature for younger people, like telling a fifty-year-old he needs to know how to use a fork. But here's the key: your blog will display you to the world. Understand what that means. Have fun with it, but do not indulge in crudity or viciousness, as other believers will have you thrown back in their faces as an example of Christian hypocrisy.

You can use cutting humor and the other weapons of argument, but be slow to do so because these are not easily mastered and can go very wrong. What you commit to your blog cannot be erased. It will follow you for as long as anyone cares to follow you, and significant people are followed very long indeed, especially by those they injure, whether rightfully or not.

The advantage of blogging is that it will oblige you to live in the world of ideas and debates, and to do so at the modern pace. At present no great blogger has emerged with a distinctly evangelical worldview. When one does, with humor and insight attached as well, that person (or persons) will have an enormous impact on the world.

Begin by studying the key blogs that are currently available, such as Instapundit (**www.instapundit.com**), the Kausfiles (**www.kausfiles.com**), the Dynamist (**www.vpostrel.com**), the Volokh Conspiracy (**www.volokh.blogspot.com**), and PowerLine (**www.powerline.blogspot.com**). After a few weeks, marry your technological ability to the form, and begin to comment on the world around you. Because blogging is the genuine marketplace of ideas, your site will prosper if you are any good. And so will your reputation—if it deserves to.

Chapter 32 from *If It's Not Close They Can't Cheat: Crushing the Democrats in Every Election and Why Your Life Depends on It* (Nashville, TN: Thomas Nelson, 2004).

CONTROLLING THE INFORMATION FLOW, PART 4: USING THE BLOGOSPHERE

When a caller to my show begins by asking, "What's a blog?" I know two things. I know he hasn't been listening long since I discuss blogs almost every day. And I know he is a low consumer of information.

High consumers of information spend a significant part of every day searching for information on whatever subject concerns them, whether it is politics, economics, stock prices, the weather, sports, or fashion. No matter what the core interests, high consumers of info are in the hunt every day and sometimes many times a day.

High consumers of info, by the way, are typically at the top of their fields because information advantage is a key to success in almost every field.

Moderate consumers of information have set up their lives to receive regular and substantial infusions of information about the topics they care about. Perhaps they take a paper or two, watch a couple of shows, listen to the radio. They are not clueless, but neither are they passionate about staying ahead of the information curve.

Low consumers of info drift along. If some information hits them in the head, it registers. If not, it doesn't.

Blogs are very much a part of the world of high-information consumers because they are the children of the internet age. If you spend much time on the web, you know about blogs.

Blog is short for "web log"—an online site with time-dated postings, maintained by one or more posters, that features links and commentary. That is the most basic definition. But it is like saying a car is a means of transportation featuring four wheels.

There are literally millions of blogs, with more being established every day. Many are started and abandoned, but most are maintained for at least a few months. My own blog, Hugh Hewitt.com, was launched in early 2002 and averages more than 5,000 visitors a day. It passed its 2 millionth visitor in early 2004.

HughHewitt.com is a relatively new and moderately successful blog. I use it to bring my readers' and listeners' attentions to stories that I judge to be important, and to circulate my commentary on those stories as well as any other subject on which I choose to opine. HughHewitt.com is my own opinion page with a readership greater than most small town dailies.

My blog is part of the political blog universe in which there are thousands of entries. The most important, given the volume of visitors and the "echo" they produce in the blogosphere at this writing, are Instapundit.com and AndrewSullivan.com, but there are perhaps fifty that matter a great deal in the world of politics. I include a current list of a few center Right blogs that beginners might want to sample in Appendix H. You need to start reading these blogs, and you need to start your own if you wish to be an effective participant in the world of politics and in the cause of destroying the power of the Democratic Party. Blogging is one field of contest between liberals and conservatives, one field of competition between Democrats and Republicans.

It is not the most important field by far, but it does matter. The blogosphere—which is the name given to the entire internet community of blogs—is part of the infrastructure by which political ideas are developed and communicated. Blogs are like small radio stations or small circulation newspapers: they are influencers of opinion.

The better the blog, the more readers it attracts. The more the readers, the more widespread the dissemination of the opinions contained on the blog.

It is that simple.

The political region of the blogosphere is credited with two major stories in recent years—the toppling of Trent Lott as majority leader and the ouster of Howell Raines as editor in chief of the *New York Times*.

Both claims have been disputed, but both have their defenders. In each instance, stories were developed on various blogs and grew in importance via repetition and elaboration until the mainstream, elite press took note and began to follow the stories with vigor. Media frenzies developed—firestorms, really, or what I took to calling "opinion storms." When such an opinion storm develops, almost every corner of media gets involved, and the stories take on a life and momentum of their own.

In the case of Howell Raines, the blogosphere provided a home for two of his most acidic and talented critics—Andrew Sullivan, who writes at AndrewSullivan.com, and Mickey Kaus, who writes Kausfiles for the online journal *Slate* (kausfiles.com). When word began to break that a young *New York Times* reporter, Jayson Blair, had lied about his sources and his stories, Sullivan and Kaus jumped on the story and drove it farther almost daily. Soon other websites were in the hunt, and a chorus of indignation arose, which flowed into other newspapers and throughout the institutions of American political power.

Each day brought new details, and Sullivan and Kaus became must-reads for everyone interested in the scandals at the *Times*. Both writers speculated whether big boss Raines—an imperious and hard Left-leaning aristocrat—could survive the revelations about the slipshod way in which he had managed not only Blair's career but also the entire news operation. Others joined in the speculation, and a critical mass of opinion was generated that the great beacon of American journalism could not regain its reputation as long as Raines remained. When his resignation arrived, it seemed in retrospect as though it had been inevitable.

But it hadn't been inevitable. Most observers agree that absent a blogosphere to fuel and drive the story, Raines would be editing the paper to this day. But with daily updates on these two sites and scores more, hunkering down was simply not an option.

Senator Trent Lott of Mississippi must still be wondering what hit him. One day his leadership of the GOP in the "world's greatest deliberative body" was unchallenged, and the next he was under fire for a toast he had offered the retiring Strom Thurmond, the one-hundred-year-old senator from South Carolina who had once run for the presidency on a segregationist platform.

In making the salute to Thurmond, Lott had stated in passing that a lot of people thought the country would have been better off if Strom had won his quixotic race for the White House in 1948. While certainly a ham-handed way of paying tribute, the remark was not initially understood by the media to be an endorsement of Thurmond's long-ago repudiated segregationist views.

But the blogosphere, principally in the form of *National Review*'s group blog, The Corner, asked tough questions about Lott's rhetoric and, in doing so, cued a gang tackle of Lott. After these conservative writers exposed Lott's weakness among folks who ought to have been supporters, reporters swooped in from every corner of the country to speculate on what Lott meant and didn't mean. Lott retreated into a "no comment" mode and then began to offer up apology after apology, but the fire lit by bloggers kept burning brighter and brighter. When President Bush added his criticisms to those of practically every commentator in the country, Lott's support in the Senate broke, and in days he announced he was stepping down as majority leader. Senator Bill Frist of Tennessee replaced him, and the national Republican Party had a new and far more sympathetic national spokesman, given Bill Frist's credentials as an accomplished heart surgeon.

Again, without a blogosphere, there would have been no momentum behind the story. Trent Lott would still, in the minds of many, be the GOP's majority leader.

Speculation about what might have happened had the internet not spawned its blogs is beside the point. The world of blogs— 24/7 news and commentary coupled with a fierce accountability and instant fact-checking—exists. Both parties have entered this election season with a commitment to managing the blogosphere.

There were blogs at both GeorgeWBush.com and dean foramerica.com. Both sites also maintained a lengthy "blogroll"— a list of hundreds of other blogs recommended for visits. The blogrolls are lengthy because inclusion is easier than exclusion, and the degree of differentiation is so advanced that it just pays to make sure every conceivable "friendly" is included. The Dean campaign embraced the blogosphere in a way no other campaign ever had, and the benefits to Dean were immense, though fleeting. Here is how the *New York Times Magazine* captured the impact of the blogging phenomenon on the Dean campaign in a December 7, 2003, profile by Samantha M. Shapiro:

> This national network of people communicates through, and takes inspiration from, the Dean web log, or blog, where official campaign representatives post messages a few times a day and invite comments from the public. The unofficial campaign

interacts daily with the campaign in other ways as well. When Jeff Horowitz, a full-time volunteer, needs help compiling news articles that make the staff's daily internal press briefing, he e-mails a request for help to a list of supporters he has never met, asking them to perform internet news searches at certain times and then e-mail him the results. "Ten people will volunteer to give me a news summary by 8 a.m.," Horowitz explains. "People in California, which means they have to get up at 4 a.m." A number of campaign staffers are in regular contact with Jonathan Kreiss-Tomkins, 14, who lives in Sitka, Alaska. Growing up on a remote Alaskan island, Kreiss-Tomkins has become especially adept at finding pen pals and online friends, and he now uses that skill on behalf of the Dean campaign, recruiting supporters through the internet and then sending lists of e-mail addresses to the campaign.

Dean's opponents have begun to mimic the trappings of his campaign. Many of the Democratic candidates now have blogs. Even President Bush has one, though comments from the public—an essential element of Dean's blog—are not allowed. The Dean campaign tracks online contributions with the image of a baseball bat (at one point, the website added a new bat for every $1 million raised); shortly after the Dean campaign raised its first million dollars, John Kerry's campaign took up the web icon of a hammer. But Dean's internet campaign dwarfs those of his rivals. In the third quarter of 2003, Kerry raised in the vicinity of $1 million online; Dean raised more than $7 million. A typical post of the Kerry blog receives, on average, 18 comments, while Dean blog posts generally receive more than a hundred. The Dean website is visited with roughly the same frequency as the White House website.

Shapiro's tone was breathless, and it was probably her first assignment covering a presidential campaign. Every presidential campaign is full of volunteers who believe they have invented a new kind of campaign, one full of genuine passion and commitment. In truth, the Dean campaign was the Ford campaign with text messaging, e-mail, and cell phones. But it had adapted the new technology, and once a technology is in play, everyone needs to master it.

Perhaps you saw Tom Cruise's recent epic, *The Last Samurai*. Forgive me if you didn't because I have to comment on the movie's end. The very honorable samurai charge Gatling guns, and they lose. Decisively. New technologies do that to old technologies.

The internet is not a brand-new technology, but political organizing via the internet is, as is the dissemination of information via blogs. Given that blogs are here to stay, with enormous power and even greater potential, what should an activist do?

Why, master the technology, of course.

That means, first, reading the major blogs regularly for a good period of time to understand what sets some apart and gains audiences for them.

Then, having figured out the basics, launch a blog via whatever platform, like "blogspot," is then dominant. Posts all over the web explain the mechanics of getting started, but the message of this chapter is this: get started. Joe Carter at EvangelicalOutpost.com wrote a great series of posts on getting started.

It is crucial for the center Right to maintain a constant flow of new bloggers into the blogosphere because sheer numbers matter and because genuine talent will rise out of the mass of bloggers. I have on my website a blogroll, and within that blogroll I have a section devoted to the Young Justice League of America, my name for a collection of under-twenty-five bloggers with real talent accompanied by the senses of irony and humor that are essential to blogosphere success.

I have carved out this area and routinely promote it because if center Right ideas are to prosper, they need carriers much younger than I am to press them forward in the years ahead. At one time opinion punditry was confined to a handful of aging center Left columnists and talking heads who fought their way up the media food chain.

No more. Now anyone with an internet connection and some basic skills can join the fray. The talented ones gain readers and, with readers, influence. The smart bloggers who have been at it for a few years do what they can to promote the good, young talent.

A decade from now the bloggers who dominate today's traffic-monitoring sites will almost all have declined or ceased to exist. New voices will have arisen. If the center Right puts a production system into place now and nurtures it with encouragement and attention, it will have the infrastructure to continue to dominate the information dissemination phase of campaigning.

High consumers of information are always going to be out there prowling for data and opinions. The party that organizes to meet that demand wins in the long run. Blogging is an essential part of that effort.

APPENDIX B

WHAT THE BLOGOSPHERE HAS WROUGHT

Studs Terkel is a brilliant man. He listened to people and constructed oral histories of their experiences in the Great Depression, World War II, on their work, on aging. He was also an accomplished radio man, which is perhaps why he had an ear for oral history. He's 92 and still writing, and is a Distinguished Scholar in residence at the Chicago Historical Association.

If Studs Terkel were younger, he'd be the perfect fellow to conduct an oral history on the blogosphere and its impact on people's lives. Such an archive on the early history of television and radio would have been a wonderful thing to compile even as those media exploded in their start-up and high-growth years.

When I began this book, I asked readers of **HughHewitt.com** to please send me e-mails that responded to the simple questions of how often they checked **Instapundit** each day and how the blogosphere had changed their lives. I have opened the "Blogosphere Oral History" section of **HughHewitt.com** as a result of the responses and will periodically call for new submissions. I cannot reproduce all the wonderful submissions in this book, but here is a sample that should underscore for the reader the truly revolutionary change under way. For the complete file, visit the online archive.

Just getting into Blogs in the past couple weeks. PowerLine is my primary several times a day along with your site and listening to you on 1280 the Patriot here in the Twin Cities. Just starting to read Glenn and a few others.

—H. G.

Every day I check: RealClearPolitics (3x); Instapundit (5x); PowerLine (4x); Kos (1); KerrySpot (4x); Polipundit (3x); Scrappleface (1x); TechCentralStation (2x).

—J. J.

Time permitting, this is my normal schedule: No, I am NOT kidding.
30–40X daily
　　Hugh Hewitt
　　Glenn Reynolds
　　NRO Kerry Spot
　　NRO Corner
20–30X
　　BeldarBlog
　　PowerLine
　　Captain's Quarters
　　Roger L. Simon
Up to 10X daily
　　QandO
　　RealClearPolitics
　　LGF

Several times daily

    Jen Martinez

    Blackfive

    Drudge

    I Love Jet Noise

At least once daily, possibly more

    Allah

    Ace of Spades HQ

    Belmont Club

    Debka

    American Spectator

    Anti-Idiotarian Rottweiller

    WSJ Opinion Journal

Not quite daily

    Neal Boortz

    Blogs for Bush

    INDC

    Daily Pundit

    Lileks

    Iraq the Model

    Jihad Watch

    Media Research Center

    Cold Fury

    Balloon Juice

    WND

    Townhall.com

    David Limbaugh

    FrontPage

    Kausfiles

    Command Post

    Northeast Intelligence Network

Bangkok Post
Gweilo Diaries

—J. W.

You ask how many times I check Instapundit—I will check Instapundit between 10 and 15 times a day. Like most bloggers, he is in my permalinks. I very much like the analogy you are constructing with major bloggers and determining their mainstream media counterparts. A few observations:

1. Comparing Instapundit to the *New York Times* makes sense, but I wonder if there's a better fit. It seems to me the frequently-updated, high-traffic blogs that Instapundit is the prototype of are more akin to wire services than individual institutions. Perhaps it makes more sense to compare Instapundit to the Associated Press? Of course, this leaves the *New York Times* comparison open. Other possibilities for blogs as wire services include Command Post (http://www.command-post.org/), Winds of Change (http://www.windsofchange.net/), or eTalkingHead (http://etalkinghead.com/).

2. Do the various "alliances" represent conglomerate groups? Is the Northern Alliance the Knight-Ridder of the blogosphere? Do the alliances foster a commonality that you might see between member newspapers, such as the *Saint Paul Pioneer Press*, the *Kansas City Star*, and the *San Jose Mercury-News* (all Knight-Ridder papers)?

3. Lileks is the *New Yorker*, or perhaps the *Atlantic*, of the blogosphere.

His style is more expository and is always entertaining, but he can bring that style to bear on hard news subjects and really create something special in his analysis.

—W. W.

I check out instapundit.com at least twice a day on my home computer and check up on it while I'm out on my cell phone which has internet access.

As for blog analogies, I see HughHewitt.com as the *Los Angeles Times*, the paper of record on the West Coast.

I see the Fourth Rail (http://billroggio.com/) as the *Time Magazine* of the blog world, not a lot of posts (like a daily newspaper), but more detailed, in-depth posts like a magazine.

As for Blogs for Bush (http://www.blogsforbush.com/) I see the Washington Times. The conservative paper of record in Washington.

I'll call Polipundit (http://polipundit.com/), the *Dallas Morning News*. Always surprising you with some info you didn't know, but is just outside that top group of newspapers (or blogs).

—A. M.

I check Glenn literally morning, noon and night (at least).

—J. W.

I check Instapundit probably 10 or more times a day. It's always the first blog I check each morning, the last every night, and if I only have time to check one thing, I go to Instapundit.

I have quite a few that I check daily. Here they are with the estimated number of times per day I check them:

Instapundit—8 to 10

Betsey's Page—4 or 5

Hugh Hewitt (yes, really!)—4 or 5

The Corner @ National Review—4 or 5

The Kerry Spot @ National Review—2 or 3

PowerLine—2 or 3

The rest of these I check once a day, usually. Sometimes I'll skip some of them and go a day or two in between checks (but never Lileks—every day for him!):

James Lileks Bleat

Neal's Nuze

Tim Blair

Vodka Pundit

JunkYard Blog

Best of the Web

Viking Pundit

Little Green Footballs

Poli Pundit

Drudge Report

I will also ALWAYS follow a link to a Mark Steyn column. This means that I'll usually see his columns 7 or 8 times because EVERYBODY links to him. He's THE Man.

BTW, one last note. I've only recently discovered your blog, but it quickly made it onto page one of my Blogs bookmark page!

—G. J.

I began visiting Instapundit in August, becoming a regular just in time for "Rathergate." Other blogs I frequent include, yours, PowerLine, Polipundit, Captain's Quarters, The Belmont Club, and the Iowa Electronic futures market (even though it's not a blog). I average 3 hits a day on Instapundit. Before, my primary news source was Lucianne.com where I learned of a jet flying into the World Trade Center. Because I work supporting trading systems for a large multi-national bank, when I saw the 9/11 news on Lucianne, I went to the trading floor where everyone was looking at TV in horror. You see, most of us in the industry knew someone who worked in the Twin Towers that day. But I digress . . . I haven't regularly watched network news since the early 1980's. And I still look at Lucianne a couple of times a day.

Finally, because of the time constraints, it is impossible for any TV news organization to provide the in-depth coverage and analysis that satisfies my curiosity. Even when I watch a Channel discussion, I'm frustrated by the questions not answered or the points not made. In contrast, the "blogo-sphere" fills that void. I can find what I'm looking for in a short period of time. The "blogosphere" allows me to get answers and sift through the analysis very quickly. I can also read intel-ligent opposing viewpoints without having to filter through the hyperbole. In sum, I get all of my news from the internet. I analyze that news with the help of some very smart people who write blogs. Thanks.

—K. B.

I am not a blogger, just a blog-reader—a hawkish pro-choice Democrat in a bluer-than-blue borough. My daily media diet starts with the *NYT* (cover to cover) and NPR (also Imus)—then I have to counteract it with some Lucianne, Instapundit, Kaus, Drudge, Hewitt, Corner, Mark Steyn, Allahpundit, Taranto, Footballs, etc. Then it's back to the dark side with The Note, Altercation and more *NYT/Wash Post/LA Times*. Radio at night: Laura Ingraham. TV: *Hardball* etc. Whew!! I'm exhausted. I check Instaman about 10 times a day . . . bottom line: without "New Media" I would be getting about a 10th of the info and opinion I now have . . .

—D. Z.

I began to seriously track blog activity in the last 6–12 months. Prior to that I read RealClearPolitics each morning (at your suggestion), *The Wall Street Journal* opinion page, WND, and your web page.

I've advanced my morning routine to include:

Hugh Hewitt (first, last and many times in the middle of the day)

Drudge	(5–6 times a day)
Newsmax	(morning and evening)
WND	(my home page, check 3–4 times a day)
Polipundit	(3–4 times a day)
Instapundit	(1–2 times a day)
LGF	(1–2 times a day)
Blogs for Bush	(3–4 times a day)
PowerLine	(3–4 times a day)
Captain's Quarters	(1–2 times a day)

I also read:

Roger L. Simon every couple of days

Mathew Yglesias once a week (it's all I can stand!)

Talking Points Memo once a week

I read virtually every link that you have in your posts so I get a smattering of many other blogs along the way.

—A. R.

I check in with Glenn about 10 times a day. (I quit my job to spend more time with the kid, who is in school all day, so I have a lot of free time to be a Security Mom.)

Some other blogs I check every day:

Hugh Hewitt

Captain's Quarters

PowerLine

BeldarBlog

Belmont Club

Little Green Footballs

Junkyardblog

Victor Hanson

Chrenkoff

Diplomad

Tim Blair

Roger L Simon

I had never read a blog until a few months ago. Andrew Sullivan was my entry to the blogosphere, through his columns in the dead tree media. I used to check him first, but now I only visit him every couple of days or so.

One more bit of boring personal history. My parents were very active in Texas politics in the 60's and early 70's. As a kid, I attended events and hung out at campaign HQ's of LBJ, John Connally, Lloyd Bentsen, and Ben Barnes, before his political career was killed by his first scandal. (He has no credibility in Texas—I laughed out loud when I saw that CBS was using him for their anti-Bush campaign.)

I always voted Republican in Presidential races, but I still considered myself to be a Democrat, until 9/11 and its aftermath. The Demos have lost all credibility. They are not only anti-American, but they are also liars. I read your latest book, and for the first time gave money to the Republican Senatorial and Congressional Committees.

—J. S.

1. Because of blogs I know that I am not the only person who has a problem with the bias in the MSM.

2. Because of blogs I am not as frustrated with the bias I

see in the MSM. I know that several someones with a better command of the language and better typing skills will nail them.

3. I see the blogs as an antidote to the elitism in the MSM and politics in general.

4. Blogs energize both the right and the left on issues. This is good and bad. Good that the right is making their case better and using the web as a way to get that case out to the people at large. On the other hand I see that the leftists are becoming more radical as they lose ground in their control of what the general public sees of the news, and the influence on the direction of the country politically. I am afraid that the leftists will align with terrorists to destroy their common foe. I know this is an insane idea but who said the leftists are sane.

I see many years of political and social strife before the leftists are shown to the general public as toxic and deserving of being ignored and removed from positions of influence.

5. I am finishing a BS degree in Information Technology (all done over the net) to go on top of my BS in Chemical Engineering (after several years of environmental consulting work to industry, I have seen the worst of the enviros, the wasted $, the lost jobs, the lies, the deceit, etc.). I intend to start a blog of my own re: computer security for the home/home office user.

6. Blogs are a filter. We badly need a detector to filter the ridiculous stuff that is on the web. Until someone like Google comes up with a peer reviewed data algorithm program that can rate the various data by knowledgeable peers in each specialty the blogs act as somewhat of a filter to alert us to lies and deceit.

7. The blogs written by those of other political and philo-

sophical views than mine alert me to the thinking (or lack of thinking) of these people.

8. One last note: I am an atheist who votes Republican.

—D. C.

I am a baby boomer who spent over 20 years abroad helping to reach out to college students in the area of faith and values. Our 3 children were born and raised in Europe and we returned to the US several years ago to allow them to attend English speaking high school (they were in national schools there) and also to get to know "their" (our) culture.

My husband and I have been shocked and saddened by the gap between what we observe as real Americans and the media. A gap which has been widening over the past years. My husband has remarked often, "there must be someone who can hold them (the MSM) accountable," and more than once I have considered dedicating all my time to organize boycotts of advertisers in order to bring pressure upon them to report more fairly.

I have not watched network news on TV for the past 4 years unless I am checking some major storm in our area. And even then I do my best to avoid any contact with the (mostly worthless) local news (who needs to know how many cats were stranded in trees today) and any news beyond. Simply because it is so maddening and absolutely unbalanced.

My daily sources for news that matters are PowerLine Blog.com, HughHewitt.com and michellemalkin.com, with a glance at realclearpolitics.com and some of the relevant links of the day from any of those sources. I listen to your radio program as often as I can, hear parts of it almost daily.

You and other conservatives have been my lifeline to reality during these Dark Ages of media dominance. It must be incredible to have been on the front lines in helping to expose and bring the MSM down, and they are tumbling. Thank you for your courage, your persistence, your commitment to things that really matter.

I also use the internet to book almost all of our airline travel and purchase most of our (many) books. (Several years ago I ordered the last 50 copies of "The Embarrassed Believer" on bookcloseouts.com for $4 each and have gladly passed them on to others! What a great book, along with your others.)

Thank you for your work and your contributions at such a time as this.

—C. G.

Recently, I had to renew my subscription to the *Orange County Register*. I thought seriously about letting it lapse because, at least with regard to the news, I rely much more on the internet than I do the paper. I have 8 or 10 sites—including yours—that I check in the morning and then repeatedly throughout the day. Depending on the intensity of my work, I might check six or eight times with my search being expanded through links to other sites.

Sometimes, at the end of the day, I realize that I have not even removed the *Register* from my briefcase.

The advantage of the blogosphere is that its reporting of and reaction to events is almost instantaneous—whether it is from someone watching a TV news report or someone actually at the location where news is happening. Blogs also provide the advantage of what you call "swarming"—analysis from many points of view. I believe they provide a much more thorough and complete picture of news events than newspapers and weekly magazines do. I also appreciate the fact that I can provide immediate feedback to blogs via e-mails, which is a much more "user friendly" method than writing and mailing a letter to the editor.

I must admit I am a little down on the *Register* for its anti-war position and the fact that if you check the by-lines for most of its articles it is almost exclusively a *NY Times* and AP newspaper in Section A. However the *Times* is not an alternative and the *Press-Enterprise* is still a small town paper.

I also worry that my selection of blogs only gives me one side of the news. However, almost all the blogs I check—the exception being Lucianne.com—not only present information from both sides, but link to other opinions on the news. I am fairly certain that if a "liberal" site raises a bona fide issue, I will be linked to it via my conservative web-sites.

I teach American Government and Politics at a local community college. The first night of class I now steer my students to the blogosphere as a source of news. Most are unfamiliar with it, but I consistently get comments from them, once they have checked it out, that it is a whole new world of information for them. I think the blogosphere has changed the world of news reporting, and politics for good.

In the end, I resubscribed to the *Register* because it has a decent Sports section and good comics. Also, I enjoy doing the crosswords.

—S. C.

We scope out locations of internet cafes first whenever we travel anywhere in the country or the world. We will access internet sites 3 times a day when traveling.

We make sure hotels have adequate internet services. We

do watch some cable TV and it is FOX. We sometimes watch Sunday talk shows to compare the bias—having read many of the articles they are discussing long before on the sites. In other words, we know about the stories before we hear it on TV or radio!

TV watching is for old movies or history channels (have to watch this too as one is run by *New York Times* and it persists a biased view). We mostly watch C-Span, and turn off the phone-call sections. We probably already know or have read a discussion from the internet re what the speakers are talking about. We like the book reviews. I keep a list of speakers/writers I like and what they say. I read their articles on line.

We read as we always have before, but probably own most of the conservative books available out there. We read history etc. as we always have, but now we watch for the "bias" in the texts. We didn't do this before. We order only from internet sites. I like to keep a copy of book recommendations posted on sites such as yours.

We have really contributed to the coffers of the book publishers and their writers!!

We listen to talk radio all day, and probably spend 2–3 hours a day online, to find out more about what talk shows have talked about (example—I started reading Thomas Sowell after hearing him on Rush. I read everything Victor Davis Hanson writes, after hearing him speak on your show). We "listen" to radio via internet sites now.

We LOVE Mark Steyn and bookmark his site. I love Yoni and have begun a thorough research of the Middle East through internet sites and books. We go to Lucianne and Free Republic first, then hit your site and use your links to all the other bloggers and sites we like.

We are incredibly well informed and we post articles from sites to other sites that allow such discussions. We send articles to friends. We try to help our democrat friends "see the light." If we are unhappy with what a TV/radio show presents, we call or write the sponsor.

We call or write our senators or congressmen whenever we are unhappy with something they have said or done. I have faxed articles to them I found on sites. We use the e-mail or phone numbers posted by various people on the sites.

I have formed discussion groups for women and we meet monthly to discuss an issue.

All in all, we are better citizens. We get the news unfiltered first, then decide what we believe on an issue. It's as if we are in advanced academic classes all day long.

We thank Rush for getting us started, and we thank you for moving it along to a higher level. Your Christian focus, by the way, has been very inspiring, and we are back at church because of this.

—J. B.

Have become a recent, big fan of yours and the blogosphere. I started reading blogs this summer as an alternative to the cable shows (you know the whole bunch). Quickly caught on and now I check all of my favs at least 7–10 times per day. I am a corp lawyer—so as you can imagine, I consider this a great deal of investment. I found myself turning to blogs more b/c of the critical look they take on political races, issues and of course, the conventional media. I have always watched and read my news with a critical eye (and as my new wife can attest to, a loud voice), but I have now found an outlet where I can seek whether my doubts and/analysis matches up with others (who can spend a great deal of time and effort following up on hunches/ thoughts).

Moreover, I am writing you tonight from Colmar, the heart and center of Alsace-Lorraine—where I am enjoying part of my honeymoon, but am always craving the latest from the campaign and of course, the latest from my std blogs. I am enduring the French-styled keyboard to write you this so that you know that as bloggers get their due (esp after the Rather fiasco), more will probably turn to bloggers as one more chan-nel to flip through. I think this is what the conventional media is missing the most—not that more of us will turn to only bloggers, Drudge or FOX News for our news, but rather, with the advent of the new media, we will end up demanding more news from more sources. Editorial decisions concerning which news stories will be covered are no longer the province of the networks and the *NYT* and *WP*. I like to think that the face of our media and the way we receive news is changing. I like to think that as more outlets develop a sort of free market of news will ensure that more than one news story and more than one side to the news story will be covered. I think that so many in the press miss the point—conservatives weren't looking for a conservative TV cable news outlet; rather, they were looking for fairer, more news expansive outlets.

Anyway, my apologies for the long note and any poor grammar or short sentences—French-stylized keyboards are not my thing!!

—F. D.

Here are some thoughts:

I have canceled several of my print subscriptions over the years. Some time ago, I would read *WSJ*, *Newsweek*, *Forbes*,

Fortune, NY Times, etc. Today, I have very [few] print subscriptions: a local paper in Chicago and the *Economist* (so I can get access to their online edition).

I get my news by perusing the [web] two or three times a day. I look at Google news, Drudge, the *WSJ* (online edition), Townhall, the *Weekly Standard*, the *American Spectator*, NRO and occasionally the *Washington Post, NY Times,* and the BBC.

I will scan through about a dozen blogs on most days including: RealClearPolitics, Instapundit, BrothersJudd Blog, Betsy's Page, LGF, Hewitt, Malkin, Lucianne, PowerLine, Lilek, Simon, and Tim Blair. I used to like Sullivan but stopped when I found he had become a single issue voter.

I spend about two hours a day doing this on average. When I am traveling it may be less and when a subject (like Rather Gate, Iraq war etc.) interests me I may spend another hour or two.

I have not been to Europe in a while but when I do, I cannot see myself going to France, Germany, Belgium, or (now) Spain. Last year, I traded in our two German Cars (Mercedes and BMW) for Japanese models.

95% of the books I buy are from Amazon. Going into a book store and dealing with understaffed, indifferent, clerks in book stores is an experience that I avoid as much as possible.

—V. S.

If I had to sum blogging up in one word, that would be CONTEXT. The blogosphere doesn't just repeat a press release or just comment on a news story. The bloggers do research, comparing what they are now reading to what they have read from other sources, and from other points in time. This historical and multiple-source work provides the appropriate CONTEXT to news and comments we see each day. That's what's missing from most "newswire" stories.

I listen to talk radio primarily. Most of what is "piped in" during the "news" segments is just someone reading what's on the AP wire. The issue is what's contained on the AP wire. First of all, the headlines lean to the left. Secondly, the "undercut" comments lean to the left. Most importantly, they leave out the proper CONTEXT so that the audience can make an appropriate interpretation of the "story."

Example headline: Crime rate up 6%! Sounds bad. However, it's possible that crime has been on a 6-year decreasing trend, and in one year, has flattened out, and has just risen just a bit due to more active enforcement, but is still well below historical levels. The AP writer needs "news" with "impact" so they cherry pick statistics to fit their mindset (negative, anti-Republican incumbents).

The blogosphere can de-bunk these situations. If crime had been down 6%, because the police had caught more of the bad guys, the AP writer would then come up with, "Prison population grows 6%" like it's a crisis . . . The blogosphere can point out these misleading items and help the reader to put current events in the proper CONTEXT.

—S. P.

Simply put, I use the blogosphere as my first pass filter on the news.

Before the blog, there were a couple of stories in the news that made me stop and reconsider my position on a political topic. One example was in the early 80's when Dan Rather reported that "An American died in Nicaragua when his helicopter was shot down during an attack on a school" (wording approximate, not exact). I supported Reagan in his drive to turn back communism, though I really thought it was more of a delaying action or a hope for a Korea like truce rather than the fall of communism that actually happened. But if we were funding people to go attack schools, that was not the right thing to do.

I went and started to investigate what really happened in the Nicaraguan attack. What I found out was that every word was factually true, but had very little to do with reality. That the way it was presented could cause even a supporter like myself [to] question their support for the contras. The school was a Nicaragua officer's training camp/school. The helicopter was not part of the attack, but was flying in the vicinity to pick up wounded contras. The wording Rather provided was very close to a Sandinista press release about the attack. I was renewed in my support for Reagan and the contras.

Back then, all I could do was practice the maxim, "fool me once shame on you, fool me twice, shame on me" and change to ABC for my nightly news. Later my choices expanded with cable news networks like Network. Even so, the blog gives me something unique. The same sort of research I did to discredit Rather's contra story is available with almost every article I read in the blog. There are links to the sources that I can go and do my own research. I can quickly google for even more detail.

I have also found that blogs are several news cycles ahead of events in many cases. I enjoy a spirited debate on issues with a liberal friend of mine. If nothing else, it helps from either of us getting into the cocooning effect. I sent him a link to a blog that discussed the draft hoax being sent to college kids. His response was, "Bush must be in trouble if you are sending me stuff about urban legends." The next day, Kerry, Edwards and

Cleland started fueling the draft hoax in their speeches. A couple days after that, our local paper had a story on the draft hoax. Staying ahead of stories like that is what the blogs are best at if you invest the time to read them.

—J. H.

I am self employed (underemployed, really) and thus am able to spend about 2 hours a day online. I check in on a variety of sites throughout the day. I'm a very heavy user, in other words, and I blog seven days a week.

1. When I travel or don't have an internet connection handy, I feel odd. It feels like when I quit smoking and wanted a cigarette. I don't alter my travel plans. But I sometimes delay my walk by a couple of hours. It has not affected my pajama-wearing habits.

2. Blogs influence the books I buy, but not CDs. I also go to health/fitness message boards to get recommendations on vitamins, equipment, etc., before I purchase and use eopinions.com as well.

3. Blogs drive (and increase) my financial support of political causes: Swiftboat Vets, the RNC and religious rights groups. The blog entry on "what to do with $100 to support republicans" is the most strategically brilliant concept since the Contract with America and it needs to be reposted and updated regularly.

4. Blogs increase my participation in the events of the day; I do phone calls/e-mails/letters based on what I read. I send links to relevant outlets in New and Old Media (Opinion Journal.com, FOX, etc.). Blogs increase my irritation factor; I broke up my Springsteen and Raitt albums and sent them back to their record companies. Blogs can direct a sense of outrage into action.

5. I use blogs for "on the ground" info that supplements (and sometimes obliterates) info I get from Old Media. CBS and Iraq are the best examples, but it doesn't have to be political. I've got a place in the hurricane belt and I've been checking with littletinylies in Coral Gables, Babalu Blog, Florida Cracker and others to get info on what's happening in South Florida. Old media is too hysterical.

There are some ways blogs have indirectly changed me.

1. I am more skeptical of all Old Media. I stopped buying the *NYT* years ago, but I am now utterly skeptical of everyone/everything, including Fox and the *NY Post*.

2. I do more of my own research and fact checking. For instance, I started seeing the name Tom Rosenthiel of the Committee for "Excellence" in Journalism. I googled him and discovered he thought it endangered Valerie Plame's life when she was ousted by Robert Novak . . . but he threw a hissy fit because George W. Bush, Terrorist Target Number One, kept secret that he was flying to Baghdad for Thanksgiving. Or Theresa Overholt did not make a peep when Nina Tottenberg said she hoped Clarence Thomas would die but raised a ruckus when Brit Hume got an award. That sort of thing.

3. I am a very heavy consumer of news. I realize the news and information cycle is not only 24/7—it's 86400/1440, so I "consume" news, information and commentary much more often (usually by checking in with online and broadcast sources). Some of that, of course, is because we're in a war and I'm a New York City resident with a Go Bag and a week's supply of food and water stashed in the apartment.

The sites I visit are Instapundit, Allahpundit, Lileks, Hugh Hewitt, INDC Journal, Wizbang! PowerLine, LGF, Oh That Liberal Media, Michelle Malkin, Rightwing News, JunkYard

Blog, Kerry Haters, Swiftboat Vets, Ace, the Belmont Club and of course, NRO's The Corner. Humor sites I visit daily are Iowahawk (a brilliant satirist), scrappleface, it comes in pints, Communists for Kerry and Blame Bush. Cox and Forkum, there's a handful of military/Iraq blogs I visit as well. I like photoshop humor so I go to fark, ted rall is full of crap, and acepilots occasionally—his map of the blogosphere should be a poster.

—V. A.

ACKNOWLEDGMENTS

Many hands made for light work. And very great speed.

Sondra Beck, Chase Exon, Justin Regele, Jeff Schermerhorn, and Kirk Winslow all helped with the research and editing of the book. All of its flaws belong to me; they share any credit it receives.

Lynne Chapman, my assistant now for fifteen years, has once again shepherded the manuscript from start to finish even as she kept all the other plates spinning!

Sealy and Curtis Yates again provided the guidance and encouragement that experienced and trusted agents do. Jonathan Merkh, Kyle Olund, and Brian Hampton of Thomas Nelson contributed great editing and encouragement. Three Hewitts—Diana, Will, and Jamie—kept eyes on the manuscript, and Snow Philip reprised her copyediting tasks, making her and my wife, Betsy, the consistent presence through all six of my books.

The book is a product of my blog, which was a product of the radio show, and the radio show is a product of many hands.

The day-to-day producing and engineering of Duane Patterson—also a fine blogger at **radioblogger.com**—and Adam Ramsey are extraordinary. Jennie O'Hagan continues to bring news affiliates and new listeners. The assistance of Michael Nolf, Alex Caudana, Austen Swaim, Ramin Ahadi, Evan Simon, and Anthony Ochoa are also appreciated.

Once again I want to point out the dream team of public-policy professionals who manage Salem Communications' News and Public Affairs Department. Russ Hauth, Russell Shubin, Ted Atsinger, and David Spady help keep Salem's message clear and convincing. Greg Anderson, Joe Davis, and a legion of station executives have built platforms from which that message can be sent. Ed Atsinger and Stuart Epperson had the vision and skill to bring all these people and hundreds more into the project of building a profitable communications company with a purpose worth pursuing.

Chapman University and its law school remain places of great innovation and talent. Many thanks to Jim Doti and Parham Williams especially, and to many faculty colleagues generally, for creating one of the rare islands in academia where conservatives can flourish. Two of my colleagues there, John Eastman and Tom Bell, are also on the leading edge of the new media revolution, which should make Chapman Law a center of innovation for years to come.

Some of these chapters began as columns for **WorldNet Daily.com** and the **WeeklyStandard.com**. Tom Ambrose and Jonathan Last are fine editors, whose encouragement has been crucial. JVL, especially, has welcomed the unexpected and the unusual. Terry Eastland has been my friend for twenty years, and his work as publisher of the *Weekly Standard* is a service to everyone who contributes there, especially me.

Bill Lobdell and Mark Roberts—one old media superstar and one new media superstar—have both debated the ideas in this book with me, each helping me to refine my arguments, even when they disagreed, sometimes forcefully.

And Betsy, as always, has kept smiling and kept her eye on the most important things, even when the writing, the blogging, the teaching, and the talking made the days crowded. For twenty-two years, she has been my editor in chief, and I hope and pray that our partnership never does anything but grow longer and better with the years. I wrote this very thing in the last book, and I hope it will mark every volume in the future if more arrive.

ABOUT THE AUTHOR

Hugh Hewitt is the host of a nationally syndicated radio show heard in more than seventy cities nationwide, and a Professor of Law at Chapman University Law School, where he teaches Constitutional Law. He is the *New York Times* best-selling author of *If It's Not Close, They Can't Cheat*. He has written four other books, including *Blog*. Hewitt has received three Emmys during his decade of work as cohost of the PBS Los Angeles affiliate KCET's nightly news and public affairs show *Life & Times*. He is a weekly columnist for *The Daily Standard*, the online edition of *The Weekly Standard*, and a weekly columnist for WorldNet Daily.com. He can be reached at **hugh@hughhewitt.com**.